THE PARADOX OF GOODNESS AND EVIL

Understanding Free Will and Human Choice

Dr. Maxwell Shimba

Shimba Publishing LLC

TABLE OF CONTENTS

PREFACE

The question of why a good God allows evil to exist in the world is one of the most profound and challenging inquiries in theology and philosophy. This book aims to explore this complex issue from a Christian perspective, delving into the nature of God, the concept of free will, and the human capacity for moral choice. Through a comprehensive examination of biblical teachings, theological insights, and practical reflections, we seek to provide a deeper understanding of the paradox of goodness and evil.

The coexistence of a benevolent, omnipotent God and the presence of evil in the world has puzzled theologians, philosophers, and believers for centuries. It raises fundamental questions about the character of God, the purpose of creation, and the role of human beings in the divine plan. This book is an attempt to engage with these questions, not merely as abstract concepts, but as issues that profoundly impact our faith and understanding of the world.

In exploring this topic, we begin with the biblical account of creation, the fall of humanity, and the subsequent introduction of sin and evil into the world. These foundational events set the stage for understanding the complex interplay between divine sovereignty and human free will. By examining the theological implications of these concepts, we hope to illuminate how God's goodness can coexist with the reality of evil.

Throughout this book, we will also consider the role of human choice and moral responsibility. The Christian faith teaches that humans are created in the image of God, endowed with the ability to choose between good and evil. This capacity for moral decision-making is a central theme in the discussion of why evil exists and how it is addressed in the divine plan.

In addition to theological and biblical analysis, this book includes practical reflections aimed at helping believers navigate the challenges of faith in a world where evil is present. How do we trust in God's goodness when faced with suffering? How can we make sense of the injustices we see around us? These are not just academic questions, but deeply personal ones that touch the core of our spiritual lives.

Our goal in writing this book is to provide readers with a thoughtful and balanced perspective on the problem of evil from a Christian standpoint. Whether you are a theologian, a student of philosophy, or someone simply seeking to understand these difficult questions, we hope this book will offer clarity, comfort, and a deeper appreciation for the mystery of God's goodness.

Ultimately, this book is an invitation to engage deeply with the Christian faith, to explore its teachings on the nature of God and the reality of evil, and to find hope in the knowledge that God's goodness is unshakable, even in the midst of a broken world.

We invite you to join us on this journey of exploration and reflection, as we seek to understand more fully the God who is both sovereign and good, even when confronted with the hardest questions of life.

DR. MAXWELL SHIMBA

CHAPTER 01

INTRODUCTION TO THE PROBLEM OF EVIL

Definition of Evil and Its Manifestations

Evil is a multifaceted concept that has perplexed theologians, philosophers, and scholars for centuries. At its core, evil can be defined as the absence or perversion of good. It manifests in various forms, from moral and natural evils to metaphysical aspects that challenge our understanding of existence and morality.

Biblical Definition of Evil

The Bible provides several insights into the nature and definition of evil. The Hebrew word for evil, "רַע" (ra), and the Greek word "κακός" (kakos) are used throughout the scriptures to describe actions, behaviors, and phenomena that are contrary to God's will and nature.

Moral Evil

Moral evil refers to actions or behaviors that result from human choices and intentions, leading to harm, suffering, or injustice. This type of evil is rooted in free will and the capacity to choose between right and wrong.

Natural Evil

Natural evil encompasses the suffering and harm that result from natural processes and events, such as earthquakes, diseases, and natural disasters. These occurrences are not directly caused by human actions but are often seen as part of the fallen world's condition.

Metaphysical Evil

Metaphysical evil involves the limitations and imperfections inherent in the created order. It encompasses the broader existential challenges and the tension between the finite nature of creation and the infinite nature of God.

Biblical Manifestations of Evil

The Fall of Lucifer

The origin of evil is often traced back to the fall of Lucifer, an angel who rebelled against God. Isaiah 14:12-15 and Ezekiel 28:12-17 describe the pride and rebellion of Lucifer, leading to his expulsion from heaven and the introduction of evil into the created order.

- Isaiah 14:12-15 (KJV): "How art thou fallen from heaven, O Lucifer, son of the morning! how art thou cut down to the ground, which didst weaken the nations! For thou hast said in thine heart, I will ascend into heaven, I will exalt my throne above the stars of God: I will sit also upon the mount of the congregation, in the sides of the north: I will ascend above the heights of the clouds; I will be like the most High. Yet thou shalt be brought down to hell, to the sides of the pit."

The Fall of Humanity

The story of Adam and Eve in Genesis 3 provides a foundational narrative for understanding moral evil. Their disobedience to God's command not to eat from the tree of the knowledge of good and evil introduced sin and death into the world, affecting all of creation.

- Genesis 3:1-6 (KJV): "Now the serpent was more subtil than any beast of the field which the LORD God had made. And he said unto the woman, Yea, hath God said, Ye shall not eat of every tree of the garden? And the woman said unto the serpent, We may eat of the fruit of the trees of the garden: But of the fruit of the tree which is in the midst of the garden, God hath said, Ye shall not eat of it, neither shall ye touch it, lest ye die. And the serpent said unto the woman, Ye shall not surely die: For God doth know that in the day ye eat thereof, then your eyes shall be opened, and ye shall be as gods, knowing good and evil. And when the woman saw that the tree was good for food, and that it was pleasant to the eyes, and a tree to be desired to make one wise, she took of the fruit thereof, and did eat, and gave also unto her husband with her; and he did eat."

The Spread of Wickedness

After the fall, humanity's propensity for evil became evident. The story of Cain and Abel in Genesis 4 illustrates the manifestation of moral evil through jealousy and murder.

- Genesis 4:8 (KJV): "And Cain talked with Abel his brother: and it came to pass, when they were in the field, that Cain rose up against Abel his brother, and slew him."

The Flood

As human wickedness increased, God decided to cleanse the earth with a flood, sparing only Noah and his family. This event underscores the pervasive nature of moral evil and God's response to it.

- Genesis 6:5-7 (KJV): "And God saw that the wickedness of man was great in the earth, and that every imagination of the thoughts of his heart was only evil continually. And it repented the LORD that he had made man on the earth, and it grieved him at his heart. And the LORD said, I will destroy man whom I have created from the face of the earth; both man, and beast, and the creeping thing, and the fowls of the air; for it repenteth me that I have made them."

Theodicy: Addressing the Paradox of Evil

God's Sovereignty and Human Free Will

The presence of evil in the world raises questions about God's sovereignty and goodness. The doctrine of free will suggests that God granted humans the ability to choose, making them responsible for their actions.

- Deuteronomy 30:19 (KJV): "I call heaven and earth to record this day against you, that I have set before you life and death, blessing and cursing: therefore choose life, that both thou and thy seed may live."

God's Purpose in Allowing Evil

While evil and suffering are often seen as antithetical to a good and loving God, the Bible provides insight into God's purposes. Suffering can lead to growth, refinement, and a deeper reliance on God.

- Romans 5:3-5 (KJV): "And not only so, but we glory in tribulations also: knowing that tribulation worketh patience; And patience, experience; and experience, hope: And hope maketh not ashamed; because the love of God is shed abroad in our hearts by the Holy Ghost which is given unto us."

The Promise of Redemption

The ultimate answer to the problem of evil is found in the redemptive work of Jesus Christ. Through His life, death, and resurrection, Jesus conquered sin and death, offering hope and restoration to a fallen world.

- John 3:16 (KJV): "For God so loved the world, that he gave his only begotten Son, that whosoever believeth in him should not perish, but have everlasting life."

Comprehensive Commentary and Analysis

Strong's Concordance Insights

Strong's Concordance provides an exhaustive list of occurrences and meanings of the words translated as "evil" in the Bible. For example, "ra" (Strong's H7451) appears numerous times, often describing calamity or moral wickedness.

Expository Study

An expository study of key passages reveals deeper theological insights. For instance, Genesis 3 not only narrates the fall but also introduces the protoevangelium, the first gospel promise in Genesis 3:15, indicating God's plan for redemption.

- Genesis 3:15 (KJV): "And I will put enmity between thee and the woman, and between thy seed and her seed; it shall bruise thy head, and thou shalt bruise his heel."

Theological Perspectives

Theologians have long debated the nature of evil and God's role in permitting it. Augustine's concept of "privatio boni" (privation of good) suggests that evil is not a substance but rather the absence of good. This aligns with the biblical portrayal of evil as a deviation from God's perfect will.

Practical Reflections

Understanding the nature of evil and its manifestations encourages believers to trust in God's ultimate plan and remain steadfast in faith. It also calls for a response of compassion and action against injustices, reflecting God's love in a broken world.

Historical and Philosophical Perspectives on Evil

The concept of evil has been a subject of profound inquiry across different eras and cultures. Philosophers and theologians have grappled with its definition, origin, and implications. In this chapter, we will explore historical and philosophical perspectives on evil, using biblical references and expository study to provide a comprehensive understanding.

Historical Perspectives on Evil

Ancient Near Eastern Views

In the ancient Near Eastern context, evil was often understood as a disruption of cosmic order. Many ancient cultures believed in a dualistic struggle between good and evil forces. For instance, in Zoroastrianism, there is a clear dichotomy between Ahura Mazda (the good deity) and Angra Mainyu (the evil spirit).

Biblical Perspective

The Bible provides a unique narrative on the origin and nature of evil. Unlike the dualistic views of other ancient cultures, the Bible presents God as the sole creator who declared His creation "very good" (Genesis 1:31). Evil entered the world through the disobedience of humanity, influenced by the serpent (Satan).

- Genesis 3:1-6 (KJV): "Now the serpent was more subtil than any beast of the field which the LORD God had made. And he said unto the woman, Yea, hath God said, Ye shall not eat of every tree of the garden?...And when the woman saw that the tree was good for food, and that it was pleasant to the eyes, and a tree to be desired to make one wise, she took of the fruit thereof, and did eat, and gave also unto her husband with her; and he did eat."

Greco-Roman Thought

Greek philosophers like Plato and Aristotle viewed evil as a result of ignorance and imbalance. For Plato, evil was the absence of good, much like darkness is the absence of light. Aristotle saw evil as a deficiency in virtue, where moral failings resulted from a lack of balance in character traits.

Medieval Theological Perspectives

Medieval theologians like Augustine and Thomas Aquinas provided significant insights into the nature of evil. Augustine's concept of "privatio boni" (privation of good) argued that evil is not a substance but a lack or corruption of good. This aligns with the biblical view that God did not create evil, but it emerged from the misuse of free will.

- Augustine, "Confessions" (Book VII): "For evil has no positive nature; but the loss of good has received the name 'evil.'"

Reformation and Enlightenment Views

During the Reformation, theologians like Martin Luther and John Calvin emphasized the sovereignty of God over all creation, including evil. They grappled with the tension between God's sovereignty and human responsibility. The Enlightenment brought a shift towards human reason and autonomy, with philosophers like Leibniz arguing that this world, despite its evils, is the "best of all possible worlds."

Philosophical Perspectives on Evil

The Problem of Evil

Philosophers have long debated the problem of evil, often phrased as a challenge to the existence of an omnipotent, omnibenevolent God. This problem is typically articulated through three propositions:

1. God is all-powerful.

2. God is all-good.

3. Evil exists.

Theodicy: Justifying God's Goodness

A theodicy attempts to reconcile the existence of evil with the goodness of God. Various approaches include:

Augustinian Theodicy

Augustine argued that God created the world ex nihilo (out of nothing) and declared it good. Evil entered through the free will of angels and humans. Thus, moral evil is a result of free will, and natural evil is a consequence of the fallen state of creation.

- Genesis 1:31 (KJV): "And God saw every thing that he had made, and, behold, it was very good."

Irenaean Theodicy

Irenaeus suggested that evil and suffering are necessary for spiritual growth and development. Humans are created in the image of God but must grow into His likeness through experiences, including suffering.

- James 1:2-4 (KJV): "My brethren, count it all joy when ye fall into divers temptations; Knowing this, that the trying of your faith worketh patience. But let patience have her perfect work, that ye may be perfect and entire, wanting nothing."

Free Will Defense

Philosophers like Alvin Plantinga have developed the Free Will Defense, arguing that God values free will so highly that He allows for the possibility of evil. Without free will, humans would be mere automatons, incapable of genuine love or moral decisions.

- Deuteronomy 30:19 (KJV): "I call heaven and earth to record this day against you, that I have set before you life and death, blessing and cursing: therefore choose life, that both thou and thy seed may live."

Soul-Making Theodicy

John Hick proposed the Soul-Making Theodicy, which posits that life's challenges and evils are necessary for soul development. This perspective aligns with the biblical view that trials and tribulations can produce character and hope.

- Romans 5:3-5 (KJV): "And not only so, but we glory in tribulations also: knowing that tribulation worketh patience; And patience, experience; and experience, hope: And hope maketh not ashamed; because the love of God is shed abroad in our hearts by the Holy Ghost which is given unto us."

Expository Study with Exhaustive Strong's Concordance

Understanding Key Terms

Using Strong's Concordance, we delve into the Hebrew and Greek terms for evil:

- Hebrew: "רַע" (ra)

  - Strong's H7451: Often used to describe anything harmful, wicked, or of bad quality.

    - Example: Genesis 6:5 (KJV): "And God saw that the wickedness [ra] of man was great in the earth, and that every imagination of the thoughts of his heart was only evil continually."

  - Greek: "κακός" (kakos)

    - Strong's G2556: Used in the New Testament to denote bad, wicked, or morally evil actions.

      - Example: Romans 12:21 (KJV): "Be not overcome of evil [kakos], but overcome evil with good."

Comprehensive Commentary

A detailed expository study reveals the multi-dimensional nature of evil in the biblical narrative. For instance, in Job, we see the complexity of natural and moral evil and God's sovereignty over both.

- Job 1:21-22 (KJV): "And said, Naked came I out of my mother's womb, and naked shall I return thither: the LORD gave, and the LORD hath taken away; blessed be the name of the LORD. In all this Job sinned not, nor charged God foolishly."

Augustine and Aquinas on Evil

Augustine's reflections in "Confessions" and Aquinas' writings in "Summa Theologica" provide deep theological insights. Augustine's notion of evil as a privation of good and Aquinas' differentiation between natural and moral evil offer robust frameworks for understanding the biblical portrayal of evil.

Practical Implications

Understanding historical and philosophical perspectives on evil equips believers to navigate their faith amidst suffering and moral dilemmas. It encourages a deeper trust in God's ultimate plan and sovereignty.

Overview of Theodicy: Justifying God's Goodness Despite Evil

The presence of evil in a world created by an omnipotent, omnibenevolent, and omniscient God has been a significant theological and philosophical dilemma. This issue, known as the problem of evil, raises profound questions about the nature of God and His relationship to the world. Theodicy is the branch of theology that seeks to vindicate God's goodness and power despite the existence of evil. This chapter provides an overview of various theodicies, examining their biblical foundations, philosophical arguments, and practical implications.

The Problem of Evil

Definition and Scope

The problem of evil is often articulated through three propositions:

1. God is all-powerful.

2. God is all-good.

3. Evil exists.

These propositions appear logically incompatible: if God is all-powerful, He should be able to prevent evil; if He is all-good, He should desire to prevent evil; yet evil exists. Theodicy aims to resolve this apparent contradiction.

Types of Evil

- Moral Evil: Resulting from human actions (e.g., murder, theft).

- Natural Evil: Resulting from natural processes (e.g., earthquakes, diseases).

- Metaphysical Evil: Inherent limitations and imperfections in the created order.

Biblical Foundations of Theodicy

Creation and Fall

The Bible begins with the narrative of a good creation marred by human disobedience. God created a world that He declared "very good" (Genesis 1:31). The introduction of sin through Adam and Eve's choice led to a fallen world characterized by suffering and death (Genesis 3).

The Sovereignty and Goodness of God

Throughout Scripture, God's sovereignty and goodness are affirmed even amidst evil and suffering. God's ways and purposes often transcend human understanding (Isaiah 55:8-9). The Book of Job, for instance, explores the mystery of suffering and divine sovereignty without providing simplistic answers.

- Job 38:1-4 (KJV): "Then the LORD answered Job out of the whirlwind, and said, Who is this that darkeneth counsel by words without knowledge? Gird up now thy loins like a man; for I will demand of thee, and answer thou me. Where wast thou when I laid the foundations of the earth? declare, if thou hast understanding."

Redemptive Suffering

The New Testament emphasizes redemptive suffering. Jesus Christ's suffering and death on the cross are central to God's plan of salvation, demonstrating that God can bring ultimate good out of profound evil and suffering (Romans 5:8).

Classical Theodicies

Augustinian Theodicy

Augustine argued that God created the world good, but evil entered through the misuse of free will by angels and humans. He introduced the concept of "privatio boni" (privation of good), suggesting that evil is not a substance but a corruption or lack of good.

- Confessions, Book VII: "For evil has no positive nature; but the loss of good has received the name 'evil.'"

Irenaean Theodicy

Irenaeus proposed that humans are created immature and must grow into spiritual maturity. Evil and suffering are necessary for this growth, serving as a means to develop virtues and deepen the relationship with God.

- James 1:2-4 (KJV): "My brethren, count it all joy when ye fall into divers temptations; Knowing this, that the trying of your faith worketh patience. But let patience have her perfect work, that ye may be perfect and entire, wanting nothing."

Free Will Defense

Alvin Plantinga's Free Will Defense posits that a world with free will is more valuable than a world without it, even if free will allows for the possibility of evil. God gave humans free will to enable genuine love and moral decisions.

- Deuteronomy 30:19 (KJV): "I call heaven and earth to record this day against you, that I have set before you life and death, blessing and cursing: therefore choose life, that both thou and thy seed may live."

Soul-Making Theodicy

John Hick expanded on Irenaeus' ideas, suggesting that life's challenges and evils are necessary for soul-making. This process enables humans to grow into the likeness of God through experiences of suffering and moral decision-making.

- Romans 5:3-5 (KJV): "And not only so, but we glory in tribulations also: knowing that tribulation worketh patience; And patience, experience; and experience, hope: And hope maketh not ashamed; because the love of God is shed abroad in our hearts by the Holy Ghost which is given unto us."

Modern Theodicies

Process Theodicy

Process theologians, like Alfred North Whitehead, argue that God is not omnipotent in the classical sense but is constantly interacting with creation. God lures creation towards goodness but does not unilaterally control it. This view redefines God's power and presence in the world.

Open Theism

Open Theism posits that God does not have exhaustive foreknowledge of future free actions. This allows for genuine human freedom and posits that God works with creation in real-time, responding to human choices and actions.

- Jeremiah 18:7-10 (KJV): "At what instant I shall speak concerning a nation, and concerning a kingdom, to pluck up, and to pull down, and to destroy it; If that nation, against whom I have pronounced, turn from their evil, I will repent of the evil that I thought to do unto them."

Expository Study with Exhaustive Strong's Concordance

Understanding Key Terms

- Hebrew: "רַע" (ra) (Strong's H7451): Often used to describe anything harmful, wicked, or of bad quality.

- Genesis 6:5 (KJV): "And God saw that the wickedness [ra] of man was great in the earth, and that every imagination of the thoughts of his heart was only evil continually."

- Greek: "κακός" (kakos) (Strong's G2556): Used in the New Testament to denote bad, wicked, or morally evil actions.

- Romans 12:21 (KJV): "Be not overcome of evil [kakos], but overcome evil with good."

Expository Analysis

A detailed expository study of key passages provides insight into the nature of evil and God's response. For example, the Book of Job addresses the complexity of suffering, emphasizing God's sovereignty and the mystery of His ways.

- Job 42:1-3 (KJV): "Then Job answered the LORD, and said, I know that thou canst do every thing, and that no thought can be withholden from thee. Who is he that hideth counsel without knowledge? therefore have I uttered that I understood not; things too wonderful for me, which I knew not."

Practical Reflections

Understanding theodicy equips believers to navigate their faith amidst suffering and moral dilemmas. It encourages trust in God's ultimate plan and inspires a response of compassion and action against injustices, reflecting God's love in a broken world.

Faith and Trust

Believers are called to trust in God's goodness and sovereignty, even when faced with inexplicable suffering and evil. The biblical narrative provides numerous examples of individuals who maintained their faith in the midst of trials.

- Proverbs 3:5-6 (KJV): "Trust in the LORD with all thine heart; and lean not unto thine own understanding. In all thy ways acknowledge him, and he shall direct thy paths."

Response to Evil

Christians are called to actively oppose evil and promote good. This involves personal moral integrity, social justice, and practical acts of kindness and compassion.

- Micah 6:8 (KJV): "He hath shewed thee, O man, what is good; and what doth the LORD require of thee, but to do justly, and to love mercy, and to walk humbly with thy God?"

Theodicy addresses one of the most challenging questions in theology: how to reconcile the existence of evil with the goodness and power of God. By exploring various theodicies, believers can gain a deeper understanding of God's nature and His purposes. This chapter has provided an overview of historical, classical, and modern theodicies, supported by biblical references and expository analysis. The journey through the problem of evil continues in subsequent chapters, offering further insights and practical guidance for faith in a world marked by suffering and moral complexity.

CHAPTER 02

THE NATURE OF GOD

Attributes of God: Omniscience, Omnipotence, and Omnibenevolence

Understanding the nature of God is fundamental to theology and the study of divine attributes. Among God's many attributes, three are particularly significant in the context of the problem of evil: omniscience (all-knowing), omnipotence (all-powerful), and omnibenevolence (all-good). This chapter will explore these attributes through biblical references, expository study, and comprehensive commentary, utilizing Strong's Concordance for deeper insight.

Omniscience: God's All-Knowing Nature

Definition and Scope

Omniscience means that God has complete and perfect knowledge of all things, past, present, and future. Nothing is hidden from Him, and His knowledge is not limited by time or space.

Biblical Foundations

- Psalm 139:1-4 (KJV): "O LORD, thou hast searched me, and known me. Thou knowest my downsitting and mine uprising, thou understandest my thought afar off. Thou compassest my path and my lying down, and art acquainted with all my ways. For there is not a word in my tongue, but, lo, O LORD, thou knowest it altogether."

- Isaiah 46:9-10 (KJV): "Remember the former things of old: for I am God, and there is none else; I am God, and there is none like me, Declaring the end from the beginning, and from ancient times the things that are not yet done, saying, My counsel shall stand, and I will do all my pleasure."

Expository Study

Using Strong's Concordance, the Hebrew word for "know" in Psalm 139:1 is "יָדַע" (yada), Strong's H3045, indicating intimate, personal knowledge. This depth of knowledge implies God's complete awareness and understanding of every aspect of creation.

Theological Implications

God's omniscience ensures that His plans and purposes are perfectly informed. He knows every possible outcome and contingency, and nothing takes Him by surprise. This attribute provides believers with confidence in God's perfect wisdom and guidance.

Practical Reflections

God's omniscience means that He understands our struggles and needs intimately. Believers can trust in His knowledge and seek His guidance, knowing that He is fully aware of their circumstances.

Omnipotence: God's All-Powerful Nature

Definition and Scope

Omnipotence refers to God's unlimited power and ability to do anything that is consistent with His nature. This attribute underscores God's supreme authority and capability over all creation.

Biblical Foundations

- Genesis 18:14 (KJV): "Is any thing too hard for the LORD? At the time appointed I will return unto thee, according to the time of life, and Sarah shall have a son."

- Jeremiah 32:17 (KJV): "Ah Lord GOD! behold, thou hast made the heaven and the earth by thy great power and stretched out arm, and there is nothing too hard for thee."

- Revelation 19:6 (KJV): "And I heard as it were the voice of a great multitude, and as the voice of many waters, and as the voice of mighty thunderings, saying, Alleluia: for the Lord God omnipotent reigneth."

Expository Study

The Hebrew word for "hard" in Genesis 18:14 is "פָּלָא" (pala), Strong's H6381, meaning to be wonderful or extraordinary. This emphasizes that nothing is beyond God's extraordinary power.

Theological Implications

God's omnipotence guarantees that He can accomplish His will and purposes. It provides assurance that no promise of God will fail and that He has the power to intervene in human history and individual lives.

Practical Reflections

Believers can rely on God's omnipotence for strength and courage in difficult times. Knowing that God is all-powerful encourages faith and perseverance, trusting that He is able to do exceedingly abundantly above all that we ask or think (Ephesians 3:20).

Omnibenevolence: God's All-Good Nature

Definition and Scope

Omnibenevolence means that God is perfectly good and loving. His actions are always in accordance with His nature of goodness, and He seeks the ultimate good of His creation.

Biblical Foundations

- Psalm 145:9 (KJV): "The LORD is good to all: and his tender mercies are over all his works."

- 1 John 4:8 (KJV): "He that loveth not knoweth not God; for God is love."

- James 1:17 (KJV): "Every good gift and every perfect gift is from above, and cometh down from the Father of lights, with whom is no variableness, neither shadow of turning."

Expository Study

The Greek word for "love" in 1 John 4:8 is "ἀγάπη" (agape), Strong's G26, indicating unconditional, selfless love. This type of love is central to God's nature and actions.

Theological Implications

God's omnibenevolence assures that His intentions towards creation are always good. Even when faced with suffering and evil, believers can trust in God's ultimate goodness and His redemptive purposes.

Practical Reflections

God's omnibenevolence calls believers to reflect His love and goodness in their lives. Understanding that God is good encourages gratitude, worship, and a commitment to living out His love in relationships and communities.

Comprehensive Commentary

Interrelation of Attributes

God's omniscience, omnipotence, and omnibenevolence are not isolated attributes but interrelated. His perfect knowledge informs His powerful actions, which are guided by His infinite goodness. This holistic understanding of God's nature helps believers navigate the complexities of life with confidence in His character.

Biblical Examples

- Joseph's Story: Joseph's life illustrates how God's omniscience, omnipotence, and omnibenevolence work together. Despite the evil intentions of his brothers, God used their actions for a greater good (Genesis 50:20).

- Genesis 50:20 (KJV): "But as for you, ye thought evil against me; but God meant it unto good, to bring to pass, as it is this day, to save much people alive."

Doctrinal Insights

The doctrines of God's attributes underpin many aspects of Christian theology, including salvation, providence, and eschatology. Recognizing God's all-encompassing knowledge, power, and goodness helps believers understand His ultimate plan for redemption and restoration.

Biblical Foundations of God's Goodness

The goodness of God is a central theme throughout the Bible, providing a foundation for understanding His nature and His interactions with humanity. This chapter will explore the biblical foundations of God's goodness through various scriptures, expository study, and detailed analysis using Strong's Concordance.

The Nature of God's Goodness

Definition of Goodness

God's goodness refers to His moral excellence, kindness, and benevolent actions towards His creation. It encompasses His love, mercy, grace, and justice.

Biblical Foundations

The Bible consistently affirms God's goodness, often associating it with His other attributes such as love and faithfulness.

- Psalm 34:8 (KJV): "O taste and see that the LORD is good: blessed is the man that trusteth in him."

- Psalm 100:5 (KJV): "For the LORD is good; his mercy is everlasting; and his truth endureth to all generations."

- James 1:17 (KJV): "Every good gift and every perfect gift is from above, and cometh down from the Father of lights, with whom is no variableness, neither shadow of turning."

Expository Study with Strong's Concordance

Using Strong's Concordance, we can delve into the original Hebrew and Greek terms translated as "good."

- Hebrew: "טוֹב" (tov)

    - Strong's H2896: This term is used to describe that which is good, pleasant, or agreeable.

    - Example: Genesis 1:31 (KJV): "And God saw every thing that he had made, and, behold, it was very good [tov]. And the evening and the morning were the sixth day."

    - Greek: "ἀγαθός" (agathos)

    - Strong's G18: This term denotes goodness, benevolence, and moral excellence.

    - Example: Matthew 19:17 (KJV): "And he said unto him, Why callest thou me good [agathos]? there is none good but one, that is, God: but if thou wilt enter into life, keep the commandments."

Expressions of God's Goodness

Creation

God's goodness is evident from the very beginning of the Bible. The creation narrative in Genesis repeatedly emphasizes the goodness of God's works.

- Genesis 1:31 (KJV): "And God saw every thing that he had made, and, behold, it was very good. And the evening and the morning were the sixth day."

Provision and Sustenance

God's goodness is also shown through His provision and sustenance of His creation. He provides for the needs of all living things.

- Psalm 145:15-16 (KJV): "The eyes of all wait upon thee; and thou givest them their meat in due season. Thou openest thine hand, and satisfiest the desire of every living thing."

Covenantal Faithfulness

God's goodness is particularly evident in His covenantal relationships. He is faithful to His promises and shows steadfast love to His people.

- Exodus 34:6 (KJV): "And the LORD passed by before him, and proclaimed, The LORD, The LORD God, merciful and gracious, longsuffering, and abundant in goodness and truth."

Salvation and Redemption

The ultimate expression of God's goodness is found in His plan of salvation through Jesus Christ. God's goodness is manifested in His grace, mercy, and love towards sinners.

- John 3:16 (KJV): "For God so loved the world, that he gave his only begotten Son, that whosoever believeth in him should not perish, but have everlasting life."

- Titus 3:4-5 (KJV): "But after that the kindness and love of God our Saviour toward man appeared, Not by works of righteousness which we have done, but according to his mercy he saved us, by the washing of regeneration, and renewing of the Holy Ghost."

God's Goodness in the Psalms

The Psalms are replete with declarations of God's goodness, often in the context of worship, thanksgiving, and trust.

- Psalm 23:6 (KJV): "Surely goodness and mercy shall follow me all the days of my life: and I will dwell in the house of the LORD for ever."

- Psalm 107:1 (KJV): "O give thanks unto the LORD, for he is good: for his mercy endureth for ever."

Expository Analysis

Examining the context and usage of "good" (tov) in the Psalms, we see a multifaceted understanding of God's goodness that encompasses His actions, character, and promises.

The Goodness of God in Jesus Christ

The Incarnation

Jesus Christ is the ultimate revelation of God's goodness. His life, teachings, miracles, and sacrificial death reveal God's loving and benevolent nature.

- Acts 10:38 (KJV): "How God anointed Jesus of Nazareth with the Holy Ghost and with power: who went about doing good, and healing all that were oppressed of the devil; for God was with him."

Parables and Teachings

Jesus' parables often illustrate the goodness of God, such as the parable of the Good Samaritan and the Prodigal Son.

- Luke 15:20 (KJV): "And he arose, and came to his father. But when he was yet a great way off, his father saw him, and had compassion, and ran, and fell on his neck, and kissed him."

The Cross and Resurrection

The crucifixion and resurrection of Jesus are the ultimate demonstrations of God's goodness, providing redemption and hope for humanity.

- Romans 5:8 (KJV): "But God commendeth his love toward us, in that, while we were yet sinners, Christ died for us."

God's Goodness and Human Experience

Trusting in God's Goodness

Believers are called to trust in God's goodness, especially in times of trial and uncertainty. The assurance of God's good nature provides comfort and hope.

- Romans 8:28 (KJV): "And we know that all things work together for good to them that love God, to them who are the called according to his purpose."

Reflecting God's Goodness

Christians are also called to reflect God's goodness in their lives through acts of kindness, love, and justice.

- Galatians 5:22-23 (KJV): "But the fruit of the Spirit is love, joy, peace, longsuffering, gentleness, goodness, faith, Meekness, temperance: against such there is no law."

Comprehensive Commentary

Interpreting God's Goodness

Understanding God's goodness requires interpreting it through the entirety of the biblical narrative. God's goodness is not always immediately apparent in human circumstances, but the Bible assures us of His unwavering benevolence.

Challenges to Perceiving God's Goodness

Human experiences of suffering and evil often challenge the perception of God's goodness. However, biblical testimony consistently affirms that God is good and His purposes are ultimately redemptive.

Practical Theology

Theological reflection on God's goodness leads to practical implications for faith and living. Trust in God's goodness encourages resilience, gratitude, and a commitment to embodying God's love in the world.

The biblical foundations of God's goodness are deeply woven into the fabric of Scripture, from the creation narrative to the redemptive work of Christ and the ongoing relationship between God and His people. Understanding and trusting in God's goodness is essential for a robust and vibrant faith. This chapter has explored the multifaceted nature of God's goodness through expository study and comprehensive commentary, providing a foundation for further theological reflection and practical application.

The Concept of God's Sovereignty and Human Free Will

The interplay between God's sovereignty and human free will is one of the most profound and challenging topics in theology. Understanding how God's supreme authority coexists with human autonomy is essential for grasping the nature of God and His relationship with creation. This chapter will explore the biblical foundations, theological implications, and practical reflections on God's sovereignty and human free will.

Understanding God's Sovereignty

Definition of Sovereignty

God's sovereignty refers to His supreme power and authority over all creation. It means that God is in complete control, governing all things according to His will and purpose.

Biblical Foundations

- Psalm 103:19 (KJV): "The LORD hath prepared his throne in the heavens; and his kingdom ruleth over all."

- Daniel 4:35 (KJV): "And all the inhabitants of the earth are reputed as nothing: and he doeth according to his will in the army of heaven, and among the inhabitants of the earth: and none can stay his hand, or say unto him, What doest thou?"

- Ephesians 1:11 (KJV): "In whom also we have obtained an inheritance, being predestinated according to the purpose of him who worketh all things after the counsel of his own will."

Expository Study with Strong's Concordance

Using Strong's Concordance, the Hebrew word for "ruleth" in Psalm 103:19 is "מָשַׁל" (mashal), Strong's H4910, indicating dominion and governance. This emphasizes God's authority over all aspects of creation.

Theological Implications

God's sovereignty assures that His purposes will ultimately be fulfilled, despite human actions or natural events. It provides a foundation for trusting in God's plan and His ultimate control over history and individual lives.

Understanding Human Free Will

Definition of Free Will

Free will refers to the ability of humans to make choices that are not determined by prior causes or by divine intervention. It encompasses the capacity for moral decision-making and personal responsibility.

Biblical Foundations

- Genesis 2:16-17 (KJV): "And the LORD God commanded the man, saying, Of every tree of the garden thou mayest freely eat: But of the tree of the knowledge of good and evil, thou shalt not eat of it: for in the day that thou eatest thereof thou shalt surely die."

- Deuteronomy 30:19 (KJV): "I call heaven and earth to record this day against you, that I have set before you life and death, blessing and cursing: therefore choose life, that both thou and thy seed may live."

- Joshua 24:15 (KJV): "And if it seem evil unto you to serve the LORD, choose you this day whom ye will serve; whether the gods which your fathers served that were on the other side of the flood, or the gods of the Amorites, in whose land ye dwell: but as for me and my house, we will serve the LORD."

Expository Study with Strong's Concordance

The Hebrew word for "choose" in Deuteronomy 30:19 is "בָּחַר" (bachar), Strong's H977, which signifies selecting or deciding between options. This highlights the biblical affirmation of human agency and responsibility.

Theological Implications

Human free will underscores the moral responsibility of individuals. It allows for genuine love, obedience, and moral growth, as choices are made freely rather than being predetermined.

The Interaction of Sovereignty and Free Will

Biblical Examples

The Bible provides numerous examples of how God's sovereignty and human free will interact:

- Joseph's Story: Joseph's brothers exercised their free will to sell him into slavery, but God used their actions to bring about a greater good.

- Genesis 50:20 (KJV): "But as for you, ye thought evil against me; but God meant it unto good, to bring to pass, as it is this day, to save much people alive."

- Pharaoh's Heart: Pharaoh hardened his heart against God's commands, yet the Bible also states that God hardened Pharaoh's heart to fulfill His purposes.

- Exodus 9:12 (KJV): "And the LORD hardened the heart of Pharaoh, and he hearkened not unto them; as the LORD had spoken unto Moses."

Theological Perspectives

Various theological perspectives attempt to reconcile God's sovereignty with human free will:

- Compatibilism: This view holds that God's sovereignty and human free will are compatible. God ordains all that happens, but humans still act freely within God's sovereign plan.

- Libertarian Free Will: This view emphasizes that humans have the genuine ability to choose otherwise, and God's foreknowledge does not necessitate determinism.

- Molinism: Named after Luis de Molina, this view posits that God has middle knowledge (knowledge of all possible worlds and what free creatures would do in any given circumstance) and uses this to accomplish His sovereign will while respecting human freedom.

Practical Reflections

Trust in God's Sovereignty

Believers are encouraged to trust in God's sovereignty, especially in times of uncertainty and suffering. God's control assures that His purposes are good and ultimately for the benefit of His creation.

- Proverbs 3:5-6 (KJV): "Trust in the LORD with all thine heart; and lean not unto thine own understanding. In all thy ways acknowledge him, and he shall direct thy paths."

Responsibility and Choice

Human free will means that individuals are responsible for their actions and decisions. Believers are called to make choices that align with God's will and reflect His character.

- Galatians 6:7-8 (KJV): "Be not deceived; God is not mocked: for whatsoever a man soweth, that shall he also reap. For he that soweth to his flesh shall of the flesh reap corruption; but he that soweth to the Spirit shall of the Spirit reap life everlasting."

Prayer and Divine Guidance

Prayer is a practical expression of acknowledging both God's sovereignty and human responsibility. Believers pray for guidance, wisdom, and the alignment of their will with God's purposes.

- James 1:5 (KJV): "If any of you lack wisdom, let him ask of God, that giveth to all men liberally, and upbraideth not; and it shall be given him."

Comprehensive Commentary

Balancing the Tension

The tension between God's sovereignty and human free will is not fully comprehensible but is a mystery embraced by faith. Recognizing this tension helps avoid extremes that either diminish God's control or human responsibility.

Historical Theological Insights

The Church Fathers, Reformers, and modern theologians have all grappled with this issue. Augustine emphasized God's sovereignty and grace, while Arminius stressed human free will and responsibility.

Implications for Doctrine and Life

Understanding the balance between sovereignty and free will influences doctrines such as salvation, providence, and eschatology. It also impacts practical living, encouraging a life of faith, obedience, and reliance on God's guidance.

The concept of God's sovereignty and human free will is a profound and complex theological topic. By exploring biblical foundations, theological perspectives, and practical implications, believers gain a deeper understanding of God's nature and their own responsibility. This chapter has provided a comprehensive overview, setting the stage for further exploration of how these truths impact faith and life.

God's Omnilove

The concept of God's omnilove, or His all-encompassing love, is central to understanding His nature and relationship with humanity. God's love is a foundational theme throughout the Bible, shaping the narrative of creation, redemption, and restoration. This chapter explores the biblical foundations of God's omnilove, examining its characteristics, expressions, and implications for believers.

Understanding God's Omnilove

Definition of Omnilove

Omnilove refers to God's perfect, infinite, and unconditional love that extends to all of creation. It is a love that is not limited by conditions or circumstances and is reflective of His very nature.

Biblical Foundations

- 1 John 4:8 (KJV): "He that loveth not knoweth not God; for God is love."

- John 3:16 (KJV): "For God so loved the world, that he gave his only begotten Son, that whosoever believeth in him should not perish, but have everlasting life."

- Romans 5:8 (KJV): "But God commendeth his love toward us, in that, while we were yet sinners, Christ died for us."

Expository Study with Strong's Concordance

Using Strong's Concordance, we can explore the Greek word for love, "ἀγάπη" (agape), Strong's G26. This term denotes unconditional, selfless love, which is central to understanding God's nature.

Characteristics of God's Omnilove

Unconditional and Selfless

God's love is not based on human actions or worthiness. It is given freely and without condition.

- Romans 8:38-39 (KJV): "For I am persuaded, that neither death, nor life, nor angels, nor principalities, nor powers, nor things present, nor things to come, Nor height, nor depth, nor any other creature, shall be able to separate us from the love of God, which is in Christ Jesus our Lord."

Sacrificial

The greatest demonstration of God's love is seen in the sacrifice of Jesus Christ.

- 1 John 4:9-10 (KJV): "In this was manifested the love of God toward us, because that God sent his only begotten Son into the world, that we might live through him. Herein is love, not that we loved God, but that he loved us, and sent his Son to be the propitiation for our sins."

Persistent and Faithful

God's love is steadfast and enduring, remaining faithful even when humans are unfaithful.

- Lamentations 3:22-23 (KJV): "It is of the LORD'S mercies that we are not consumed, because his compassions fail not. They are new every morning: great is thy faithfulness."

Transformative

God's love has the power to transform lives, bringing healing, redemption, and new life.

- 2 Corinthians 5:17 (KJV): "Therefore if any man be in Christ, he is a new creature: old things are passed away; behold, all things are become new."

Expressions of God's Omnilove

Creation

God's love is evident in the act of creation, where He created the world and humanity out of love and for relationship.

- Genesis 1:27 (KJV): "So God created man in his own image, in the image of God created he him; male and female created he them."

Providence

God continually sustains and cares for His creation, providing for the needs of all living things.

- Psalm 145:15-16 (KJV): "The eyes of all wait upon thee; and thou givest them their meat in due season. Thou openest thine hand, and satisfiest the desire of every living thing."

Covenantal Relationship

Throughout the Bible, God's love is expressed through His covenantal relationships with His people, marked by His faithfulness and commitment.

- Deuteronomy 7:9 (KJV): "Know therefore that the LORD thy God, he is God, the faithful God, which keepeth covenant and mercy with them that love him and keep his commandments to a thousand generations."

Redemption

The ultimate expression of God's love is seen in the redemptive work of Jesus Christ, who came to save humanity from sin and death.

- Ephesians 2:4-5 (KJV): "But God, who is rich in mercy, for his great love wherewith he loved us, Even when we were dead in sins, hath quickened us together with Christ, (by grace ye are saved;)"

Implications of God's Omnilove

Assurance and Comfort

Believers can find assurance and comfort in God's steadfast love, knowing that it is unchanging and ever-present.

- Psalm 136:1 (KJV): "O give thanks unto the LORD; for he is good: for his mercy endureth for ever."

Motivation for Love and Service

Understanding God's love compels believers to love others and serve selflessly, reflecting God's love in their actions.

- 1 John 4:11 (KJV): "Beloved, if God so loved us, we ought also to love one another."

Basis for Forgiveness and Reconciliation

God's love provides the basis for forgiveness and reconciliation, both with God and with others.

- Colossians 3:13 (KJV): "Forbearing one another, and forgiving one another, if any man have a quarrel against any: even as Christ forgave you, so also do ye."

Hope and Eternal Life

God's love assures believers of the hope of eternal life and the promise of being with Him forever.

- John 14:2-3 (KJV): "In my Father's house are many mansions: if it were not so, I would have told you. I go to prepare a place for you. And if I go and prepare a place for you, I will come again, and receive you unto myself; that where I am, there ye may be also."

Comprehensive Commentary

Interpreting Omnilove

God's omnilove is best understood through the entirety of the biblical narrative, from creation to redemption and beyond. It is a consistent theme that reveals God's character and His intentions for humanity.

Challenges and Misunderstandings

Despite the clarity of God's love in Scripture, human experiences of suffering and evil can challenge the perception of His love. However, the Bible provides assurance that God's love remains constant and redemptive, even in difficult circumstances.

Practical Theology

Reflecting on God's omnilove has profound implications for how believers live their lives. It calls for a response of love, gratitude, and commitment to living out God's love in the world.

God's omnilove is a foundational aspect of His nature, deeply woven into the fabric of Scripture. It is characterized by its unconditional, sacrificial, persistent, and transformative qualities. Understanding and embracing God's omnilove provides assurance, motivates love and service, and grounds the hope of eternal life. This chapter has explored the biblical foundations and implications of God's omnilove, providing a comprehensive understanding of this profound truth.

This chapter has laid a comprehensive groundwork for understanding God's omnilove, setting the stage for further exploration of His nature and His interaction with the world. Subsequent chapters will build on these insights, delving deeper into the theological and practical dimensions of God's love and His relationship with humanity.

CHAPTER 03

CREATION AND THE ORIGINAL GOODNESS

The Biblical Account of Creation in Genesis

The biblical account of creation, as recorded in the book of Genesis, is foundational to understanding the nature of God, the world, and humanity's place within it. This chapter explores the narrative of creation in Genesis, emphasizing the original goodness of creation and its implications for theology and life.

The Creation Narrative in Genesis

Genesis 1:1-2:3: The Seven Days of Creation

Day 1: Light and Darkness

- Genesis 1:1-5 (KJV): "In the beginning God created the heaven and the earth. And the earth was without form, and void; and darkness was upon the face of the deep. And the Spirit of God moved upon the face of the waters. And God said, Let there be light: and there was light. And God saw the light, that it was good: and God divided the light from the darkness. And God called the light Day, and the darkness he called Night. And the evening and the morning were the first day."

God's first creative act brings forth light, symbolizing the initiation of order and life. The separation of light and darkness establishes the first structure within creation.

Day 2: The Firmament

- Genesis 1:6-8 (KJV): "And God said, Let there be a firmament in the midst of the waters, and let it divide the waters from the waters. And God made the firmament, and divided the waters which were under the firmament from the waters which were above the firmament: and it was so. And God called the firmament Heaven. And the evening and the morning were the second day."

God creates the sky by separating the waters, further organizing the cosmos and preparing the environment for life.

Day 3: Land, Sea, and Vegetation

- Genesis 1:9-13 (KJV): "And God said, Let the waters under the heaven be gathered together unto one place, and let the dry land appear: and it was so. And God called the dry land Earth; and the gathering together of the waters called he

Seas: and God saw that it was good. And God said, Let the earth bring forth grass, the herb yielding seed, and the fruit tree yielding fruit after his kind, whose seed is in itself, upon the earth: and it was so. And the earth brought forth grass, and herb yielding seed after his kind, and the tree yielding fruit, whose seed was in itself, after his kind: and God saw that it was good. And the evening and the morning were the third day."

The emergence of dry land and the creation of vegetation establish the conditions necessary for sustaining life.

Day 4: Sun, Moon, and Stars

- Genesis 1:14-19 (KJV): "And God said, Let there be lights in the firmament of the heaven to divide the day from the night; and let them be for signs, and for seasons, and for days, and years: And let them be for lights in the firmament of the heaven to give light upon the earth: and it was so. And God made two great lights; the greater light to rule the day, and the lesser light to rule the night: he made the stars also. And God set them in the firmament of the heaven to give light upon the earth, And to rule over the day and over the night, and to divide the light from the darkness: and God saw that it was good. And the evening and the morning were the fourth day."

God creates the celestial bodies, establishing the rhythm of time and seasons essential for life.

Day 5: Fish and Birds

- Genesis 1:20-23 (KJV): "And God said, Let the waters bring forth abundantly the moving creature that hath life, and fowl that may fly above the earth in the open firmament of heaven. And God created great whales, and every living creature that moveth, which the waters brought forth abundantly, after their kind, and every winged fowl after his kind: and God saw that it was good. And God blessed them, saying, Be fruitful, and multiply, and fill the waters in the seas, and let fowl multiply in the earth. And the evening and the morning were the fifth day."

The creation of marine life and birds introduces the diversity of life forms that populate the earth and the skies.

Day 6: Animals and Humans

- Genesis 1:24-31 (KJV): "And God said, Let the earth bring forth the living creature after his kind, cattle, and creeping thing, and beast of the earth after his kind: and it was so. And God made the beast of the earth after his kind, and cattle after their kind, and every thing that creepeth upon the earth after his kind: and God saw that it was good. And God said, Let us make man in our image, after our likeness: and let them have dominion over the fish of the sea, and over the fowl of the air, and over the cattle, and over all the earth, and over every creeping thing that creepeth upon the earth. So God created man in his own image, in the image of God created he him; male and female created he them. And God blessed them, and God said unto them, Be fruitful, and multiply, and replenish the earth, and subdue it: and have dominion over the fish of the sea, and over the fowl of the air, and over every living thing that moveth upon the earth. And God said, Behold, I have given you every herb bearing seed, which is upon the face of all the earth, and every tree, in the which is the fruit of a tree yielding seed; to you it shall be for meat. And to every beast of the earth, and to every fowl of the air, and to every thing that creepeth upon the earth, wherein there is life, I have given every green herb for meat: and it was so. And God saw every thing that he had made, and, behold, it was very good. And the evening and the morning were the sixth day."

God's creation culminates with the creation of humans, made in His image, to have dominion over the earth and its creatures. This act signifies the unique relationship between God and humanity.

Day 7: Rest

- Genesis 2:1-3 (KJV): "Thus the heavens and the earth were finished, and all the host of them. And on the seventh day God ended his work which he had made; and he rested on the seventh day from all his work which he had made. And God blessed the seventh day, and sanctified it: because that in it he had rested from all his work which God created and made."

God's rest on the seventh day establishes the pattern of Sabbath, emphasizing rest and reflection on His completed work.

The Original Goodness of Creation

Repeated Affirmation of Goodness

Throughout the creation narrative, God repeatedly affirms the goodness of His creation. This repetition underscores the inherent value and perfection of the created order before the fall.

- Genesis 1:4 (KJV): "And God saw the light, that it was good: and God divided the light from the darkness."

- Genesis 1:10 (KJV): "And God called the dry land Earth; and the gathering together of the waters called he Seas: and God saw that it was good."

- Genesis 1:12 (KJV): "And the earth brought forth grass, and herb yielding seed after his kind, and the tree yielding fruit, whose seed was in itself, after his kind: and God saw that it was good."

Humanity's Unique Role and Goodness

The creation of humanity in God's image (Imago Dei) reflects the highest expression of His creative work. Humans are endowed with the capacity for relationship, creativity, moral decision-making, and stewardship.

- Genesis 1:26-27 (KJV): "And God said, Let us make man in our image, after our likeness: and let them have dominion over the fish of the sea, and over the fowl of the air, and over the cattle, and over all the earth, and over every creeping thing that creepeth upon the earth. So God created man in his own image, in the image of God created he him; male and female created he them."

The Very Good Declaration

The culmination of God's creative work is marked by His declaration that it was "very good."

- Genesis 1:31 (KJV): "And God saw every thing that he had made, and, behold, it was very good. And the evening and the morning were the sixth day."

This declaration signifies the completeness and perfection of creation, highlighting the harmonious and integrated nature of all created things.

Theological Implications of the Creation Narrative

The Nature of God as Creator

The creation narrative reveals God's omnipotence, wisdom, and benevolence. His power is demonstrated in His ability to create ex nihilo (out of nothing), His wisdom in the order and complexity of creation, and His benevolence in the goodness of all He has made.

- Isaiah 40:28 (KJV): "Hast thou not known? hast thou not heard, that the everlasting God, the LORD, the Creator of the ends of the earth, fainteth not, neither is weary? there is no searching of his understanding."

Human Dignity and Purpose

Being made in God's image confers intrinsic dignity and value on all humans. It also defines humanity's purpose to reflect God's character and steward His creation.

- Psalm 8:4-6 (KJV): "What is man, that thou art mindful of him? and the son of man, that thou visitest him? For thou hast made him a little lower than the angels, and hast crowned him with glory and honour. Thou madest him to have dominion over the works of thy hands; thou hast put all things under his feet."

Sabbath and Rest

God's rest on the seventh day sets a precedent for the Sabbath, emphasizing the importance of rest, reflection, and worship. It highlights the rhythm of work and rest intended for human flourishing.

- Exodus 20:8-11 (KJV): "Remember the sabbath day, to keep it holy. Six days shalt thou labour, and do all thy work:

But the seventh day is the sabbath of the LORD thy God: in it thou shalt not do any work, thou, nor thy son, nor thy daughter, thy manservant, nor thy maidservant, nor thy cattle, nor thy stranger that is within thy gates: For in six days the LORD made heaven and earth, the sea, and all that in them is, and rested the seventh day: wherefore the LORD blessed the sabbath day, and hallowed it."

Comprehensive Commentary

Interpreting Genesis 1-2

The creation account in Genesis is rich in theological meaning and symbolic significance. It provides foundational truths about God's nature, human identity, and the purpose of creation. The narrative structure, poetic elements, and repetitive affirmations emphasize the order, goodness, and intentionality of God's creative work.

Expository Insights

Using Strong's Concordance, we gain deeper insights into key terms:

- Created ("בָּרָא" bara) - Strong's H1254: This Hebrew word signifies creating something new and unique, often with divine connotations.

- Good ("טוֹב" tov) - Strong's H2896: Indicates not only moral goodness but also beauty, order, and harmony.

Practical Theology

Understanding the biblical account of creation shapes our worldview and ethics. It calls believers to respect the inherent goodness of creation, engage in responsible stewardship, and recognize the sacredness of human life.

The biblical account of creation in Genesis reveals the profound truths about God's nature, the inherent goodness of creation, and humanity's unique role within it. This narrative sets the stage for understanding the fall, redemption, and ultimate restoration of creation. By exploring the creation account, we gain a deeper appreciation of God's creative power, wisdom, and love, and are called to live in harmony with His original intent for the world.

The Original State of Goodness in the World

The biblical account of creation presents a world that was originally created in a state of perfect goodness. This chapter explores the original state of goodness in the world, as described in the early chapters of Genesis. We will examine the characteristics of this goodness, the harmony of creation, and the theological implications of this state of original goodness.

The Biblical Foundation of Original Goodness

The Creation Narrative

The creation narrative in Genesis provides a detailed account of the world's origins and its inherent goodness. Each act of creation is punctuated by God's affirmation of its goodness.

- Genesis 1:1-31 (KJV): "In the beginning God created the heaven and the earth... And God saw every thing that he had made, and, behold, it was very good. And the evening and the morning were the sixth day."

God's Affirmation of Goodness

God's repeated declaration that His creation was "good" culminates in the affirmation that it was "very good" after the creation of humanity.

- Genesis 1:31 (KJV): "And God saw every thing that he had made, and, behold, it was very good. And the evening and the morning were the sixth day."

Characteristics of Original Goodness

Order and Harmony

The original state of goodness is characterized by order and harmony. The systematic and purposeful acts of creation establish a world of balance and coherence.

- Genesis 1:2-3 (KJV): "And the earth was without form, and void; and darkness was upon the face of the deep. And the Spirit of God moved upon the face of the waters. And God said, Let there be light: and there was light."

Abundance and Provision

Creation is depicted as abundant and capable of providing for all forms of life. Vegetation, animals, and humans are all given what they need to thrive.

- Genesis 1:29-30 (KJV): "And God said, Behold, I have given you every herb bearing seed, which is upon the face of all the earth, and every tree, in the which is the fruit of a tree yielding seed; to you it shall be for meat. And to every beast of the earth, and to every fowl of the air, and to every thing that creepeth upon the earth, wherein there is life, I have given every green herb for meat: and it was so."

Relationships and Community

The original goodness also includes harmonious relationships. Humans are created for relationship with God, each other, and the rest of creation.

- Genesis 2:18-25 (KJV): "And the LORD God said, It is not good that the man should be alone; I will make him an help meet for him... And they were both naked, the man and his wife, and were not ashamed."

Theological Implications of Original Goodness

God's Nature and Creation

The original state of goodness reflects God's character. As a good and benevolent Creator, God's works naturally reflect His nature.

- Psalm 33:5 (KJV): "He loveth righteousness and judgment: the earth is full of the goodness of the LORD."

Human Dignity and Purpose

Being created in God's image confers inherent dignity and purpose on humanity. This status entails stewardship and care for creation, as well as moral responsibility.

- Genesis 1:26-28 (KJV): "And God said, Let us make man in our image, after our likeness: and let them have dominion over the fish of the sea, and over the fowl of the air, and over the cattle, and over all the earth, and over every creeping thing that creepeth upon the earth."

Sabbath and Rest

The Sabbath rest on the seventh day signifies completion and satisfaction in the goodness of creation. It establishes a pattern of work and rest that reflects God's own rest.

- Genesis 2:2-3 (KJV): "And on the seventh day God ended his work which he had made; and he rested on the seventh day from all his work which he had made. And God blessed the seventh day, and sanctified it: because that in it he had rested from all his work which God created and made."

Expository Study with Strong's Concordance

Good ("טוב" tov)

The Hebrew word "טוֹב" (tov), Strong's H2896, is used repeatedly in Genesis 1 to describe creation. It encompasses not only moral goodness but also aesthetic beauty, functionality, and completeness.

Very Good ("טוֹב מְאֹד" tov meod)

The phrase "טוֹב מְאֹד" (tov meod), Strong's H3966 and H2896, intensifies the goodness, indicating an exceptional state of well-being and harmony.

- Genesis 1:31 (KJV): "And God saw everything that he had made, and, behold, it was very good."

The Original Harmony of Creation

Harmony with God

Humans were created to live in intimate relationship with God, enjoying His presence and guidance.

- Genesis 3:8 (KJV): "And they heard the voice of the LORD God walking in the garden in the cool of the day."

Harmony with Each Other

The relationship between Adam and Eve is depicted as one of mutual support and partnership.

- Genesis 2:23-25 (KJV): "And Adam said, This is now bone of my bones, and flesh of my flesh: she shall be called Woman, because she was taken out of Man. Therefore shall a man leave his father and his mother, and shall cleave unto his wife: and they shall be one flesh."

Harmony with Creation

Humans were given the responsibility to steward and care for the earth, maintaining the balance and flourishing of creation.

- Genesis 2:15 (KJV): "And the LORD God took the man, and put him into the garden of Eden to dress it and to keep it."

Implications for Humanity Today

Environmental Stewardship

Recognizing the original goodness and harmony of creation calls for responsible stewardship of the environment. Christians are called to care for the earth, reflecting God's love for His creation.

- Psalm 24:1 (KJV): "The earth is the LORD'S, and the fulness thereof; the world, and they that dwell therein."

Restoring Relationships

The original state of goodness emphasizes the importance of healthy, supportive relationships. Efforts to restore broken relationships reflect God's original intent for harmony.

- Ephesians 4:32 (KJV): "And be ye kind one to another, tenderhearted, forgiving one another, even as God for Christ's sake hath forgiven you."

Living in Harmony with God's Will

Emulating the original harmony with God involves living in accordance with His will, seeking to embody the values of the Kingdom of God.

- Micah 6:8 (KJV): "He hath shewed thee, O man, what is good; and what doth the LORD require of thee, but to do justly, and to love mercy, and to walk humbly with thy God?"

Comprehensive Commentary

Reflecting on Original Goodness

The original state of goodness provides a paradigm for understanding God's intentions for the world. It reminds us of the inherent value of creation and the high calling of humanity as stewards of this good world.

The Impact of the Fall

While the fall disrupted the original harmony and goodness, the narrative of Genesis provides hope for redemption and restoration through God's ongoing work in the world.

- Romans 8:20-21 (KJV): "For the creature was made subject to vanity, not willingly, but by reason of him who hath subjected the same in hope, Because the creature itself also shall be delivered from the bondage of corruption into the glorious liberty of the children of God."

Practical Theology

Understanding the original state of goodness shapes Christian ethics and mission. It calls believers to engage in acts of restoration, justice, and care, aligning their lives with God's creative purpose.

The original state of goodness in the world, as described in Genesis, reveals God's intentions for a harmonious, abundant, and relational creation. This foundational truth shapes our understanding of God, humanity, and the world. It calls us to reflect on the inherent goodness of creation and our role in maintaining and restoring this goodness. This chapter has explored the biblical foundations, characteristics, and implications of the original state of goodness, providing a comprehensive understanding of this profound theological concept.

The Role of Humans as Stewards of Creation

The concept of stewardship is central to the biblical understanding of humanity's relationship with creation. From the very beginning, humans were given the responsibility to care for and manage the earth. This chapter explores the biblical foundations of stewardship, the nature and responsibilities of human dominion, and the theological and practical implications of being stewards of creation.

Biblical Foundations of Stewardship

Creation Mandate

The creation mandate given to Adam and Eve outlines the foundational role of humans as stewards of God's creation.

- Genesis 1:26-28 (KJV): "And God said, Let us make man in our image, after our likeness: and let them have dominion over the fish of the sea, and over the fowl of the air, and over the cattle, and over all the earth, and over every creeping thing that creepeth upon the earth. So God created man in his own image, in the image of God created he him; male and female created he them. And God blessed them, and God said unto them, Be fruitful, and multiply, and replenish the earth, and subdue it: and have dominion over the fish of the sea, and over the fowl of the air, and over every living thing that moveth upon the earth."

Cultivating and Keeping the Garden

God placed Adam in the Garden of Eden to cultivate and keep it, indicating a hands-on role in caring for creation.

- Genesis 2:15 (KJV): "And the LORD God took the man, and put him into the garden of Eden to dress it and to keep it."

Stewardship as Service

Stewardship is viewed as a form of service to God, involving the responsible management of the resources entrusted to humanity.

- 1 Corinthians 4:2 (KJV): "Moreover it is required in stewards, that a man be found faithful."

The Nature and Responsibilities of Human Dominion

Dominion with Responsibility

The dominion given to humans is not a license for exploitation but a call to responsible management and care for creation.

- Psalm 8:6-8 (KJV): "Thou madest him to have dominion over the works of thy hands; thou hast put all things under his feet: All sheep and oxen, yea, and the beasts of the field; The fowl of the air, and the fish of the sea, and whatsoever passeth through the paths of the seas."

Stewardship and Sustainability

Human stewardship involves ensuring the sustainability of creation, allowing it to flourish and continue providing for future generations.

- Leviticus 25:23-24 (KJV): "The land shall not be sold for ever: for the land is mine; for ye are strangers and sojourners with me. And in all the land of your possession ye shall grant a redemption for the land."

Caring for the Vulnerable

Stewardship also includes caring for the vulnerable and marginalized, both human and non-human, reflecting God's compassion and justice.

- Proverbs 12:10 (KJV): "A righteous man regardeth the life of his beast: but the tender mercies of the wicked are cruel."

- Deuteronomy 22:6 (KJV): "If a bird's nest chance to be before thee in the way in any tree, or on the ground, whether they be young ones, or eggs, and the dam sitting upon the young, or upon the eggs, thou shalt not take the dam with the young."

Theological Implications of Stewardship

Imago Dei and Stewardship

Being made in the image of God (Imago Dei) imparts a unique responsibility to reflect God's character in the care of creation. Stewardship is an expression of this image-bearing role.

- Genesis 1:27-28 (KJV): "So God created man in his own image, in the image of God created he him; male and female created he them. And God blessed them, and God said unto them, Be fruitful, and multiply, and replenish the earth, and subdue it: and have dominion over the fish of the sea, and over the fowl of the air, and over every living thing that moveth upon the earth."

Creation as God's Revelation

Creation reveals God's attributes and glory. Human stewardship involves maintaining and enhancing this revelation by preserving the beauty and integrity of the natural world.

- Psalm 19:1-2 (KJV): "The heavens declare the glory of God; and the firmament sheweth his handywork. Day unto day uttereth speech, and night unto night sheweth knowledge."

Eschatological Hope and Stewardship

Christian stewardship is motivated by the hope of new creation. Believers are called to participate in God's redemptive work, anticipating the ultimate renewal of all things.

- Romans 8:19-21 (KJV): "For the earnest expectation of the creature waiteth for the manifestation of the sons of God. For the creature was made subject to vanity, not willingly, but by reason of him who hath subjected the same in hope, Because the creature itself also shall be delivered from the bondage of corruption into the glorious liberty of the children of God."

Practical Reflections on Stewardship

Environmental Care

Practical stewardship involves active efforts to protect and sustain the environment. This includes reducing waste, conserving resources, and supporting policies and practices that promote ecological health.

- Genesis 2:15 (KJV): "And the LORD God took the man, and put him into the garden of Eden to dress it and to keep it."

Community and Stewardship

Stewardship extends to building and nurturing communities. This involves fostering relationships, promoting justice, and ensuring the well-being of all community members.

- Acts 4:32 (KJV): "And the multitude of them that believed were of one heart and of one soul: neither said any of them that ought of the things which he possessed was his own; but they had all things common."

Personal Responsibility

Each individual is called to practice stewardship in their daily lives, making choices that reflect care for creation and responsibility towards others.

- Micah 6:8 (KJV): "He hath shewed thee, O man, what is good; and what doth the LORD require of thee, but to do justly, and to love mercy, and to walk humbly with thy God?"

Expository Study with Strong's Concordance

Steward ("οἰκονόμος" oikonomos)

The Greek word "οἰκονόμος" (oikonomos), Strong's G3623, means a manager or overseer, especially one entrusted with the care of a household or estate.

- 1 Corinthians 4:2 (KJV): "Moreover it is required in stewards, that a man be found faithful."

Dominion ("רָדָה" radah)

The Hebrew word "רָדָה" (radah), Strong's H7287, means to rule or have dominion. It implies leadership with care and responsibility.

- Genesis 1:28 (KJV): "And God blessed them, and God said unto them, Be fruitful, and multiply, and replenish the earth, and subdue it: and have dominion over the fish of the sea, and over the fowl of the air, and over every living thing that moveth upon the earth."

Comprehensive Commentary

Interpreting Stewardship

Stewardship in the biblical sense is holistic, encompassing care for the environment, ethical use of resources, and fostering healthy communities. It is grounded in the understanding that all creation belongs to God and humans are caretakers.

Challenges in Stewardship

Modern challenges such as environmental degradation, climate change, and social injustice highlight the need for renewed commitment to biblical stewardship principles.

Practical Theology

Implementing stewardship principles requires practical steps such as advocating for environmental policies, engaging in community service, and promoting sustainable practices in personal and corporate life.

The role of humans as stewards of creation is a profound responsibility given by God. It encompasses caring for the environment, fostering community well-being, and living in a way that reflects God's character and intentions for His creation. By understanding and embracing our role as stewards, we participate in God's ongoing work of sustaining and redeeming the world. This chapter has explored the biblical foundations, nature, responsibilities, and practical implications of stewardship, providing a comprehensive understanding of this vital aspect of human vocation.

The Tree of Knowledge of Good and Evil

The tree of knowledge of good and evil is one of the most intriguing and significant elements in the biblical narrative of Genesis. Its presence in the Garden of Eden raises profound questions about God's intentions and the nature of human free will. This chapter explores the purpose of the tree, its role in the broader narrative, and the theological implications of its creation.

The Biblical Account

The Creation of the Tree

The tree of knowledge of good and evil is introduced as part of God's creation in the Garden of Eden, alongside the tree of life.

- Genesis 2:8-9 (KJV): "And the LORD God planted a garden eastward in Eden; and there he put the man whom he had formed. And out of the ground made the LORD God to grow every tree that is pleasant to the sight, and good for food; the tree of life also in the midst of the garden, and the tree of knowledge of good and evil."

The Command Regarding the Tree

God gives Adam a specific command concerning the tree, highlighting its significance.

- Genesis 2:16-17 (KJV): "And the LORD God commanded the man, saying, Of every tree of the garden thou mayest freely eat: But of the tree of the knowledge of good and evil, thou shalt not eat of it: for in the day that thou eatest thereof thou shalt surely die."

Purpose of the Tree

A Test of Obedience and Free Will

The tree represents a test of obedience for Adam and Eve. It provides an opportunity for humans to exercise their free will and make a conscious choice to trust and obey God.

- Genesis 2:16-17 (KJV): "And the LORD God commanded the man, saying, Of every tree of the garden thou mayest freely eat: But of the tree of the knowledge of good and evil, thou shalt not eat of it: for in the day that thou eatest thereof thou shalt surely die."

Symbol of Moral Responsibility

The tree symbolizes moral responsibility and the knowledge that comes with it. By forbidding its fruit, God sets a boundary that defines good and evil, right and wrong.

- Genesis 3:22 (KJV): "And the LORD God said, Behold, the man is become as one of us, to know good and evil: and now, lest he put forth his hand, and take also of the tree of life, and eat, and live for ever:"

Demonstration of Love and Trust

God's command regarding the tree is an expression of His desire for a relationship based on love and trust, rather than coercion. It invites humans to choose to love and trust God freely.

- John 14:15 (KJV): "If ye love me, keep my commandments."

The Fall and Its Consequences

The Temptation and Disobedience

The narrative of the fall describes how Adam and Eve, tempted by the serpent, choose to eat the forbidden fruit, leading to a fundamental change in their relationship with God and creation.

- Genesis 3:1-6 (KJV): "Now the serpent was more subtil than any beast of the field which the LORD God had made. And he said unto the woman, Yea, hath God said, Ye shall not eat of every tree of the garden?... And when the woman saw that the tree was good for food, and that it was pleasant to the eyes, and a tree to be desired to make one wise, she took of the fruit thereof, and did eat, and gave also unto her husband with her; and he did eat."

The Immediate Consequences

Eating the fruit results in the immediate awareness of their nakedness and the introduction of shame and fear.

- Genesis 3:7-10 (KJV): "And the eyes of them both were opened, and they knew that they were naked; and they sewed fig leaves together, and made themselves aprons. And they heard the voice of the LORD God walking in the garden in the cool of the day: and Adam and his wife hid themselves from the presence of the LORD God amongst the trees of the garden."

The Long-Term Consequences

The long-term consequences include pain, toil, and death, fundamentally altering the human experience and the state of creation.

- Genesis 3:16-19 (KJV): "Unto the woman he said, I will greatly multiply thy sorrow and thy conception; in sorrow thou shalt bring forth children; and thy desire shall be to thy husband, and he shall rule over thee. And unto Adam he said, Because thou hast hearkened unto the voice of thy wife, and hast eaten of the tree, of which I commanded thee, saying, Thou shalt not eat of it: cursed is the ground for thy sake; in sorrow shalt thou eat of it all the days of thy life; Thorns also and thistles shall it bring forth to thee; and thou shalt eat the herb of the field; In the sweat of thy face shalt thou eat bread, till thou return unto the ground; for out of it wast thou taken: for dust thou art, and unto dust shalt thou return."

Theological Implications

Free Will and Moral Agency

The existence of the tree underscores the importance of free will and moral agency. Humans are not mere automatons but are endowed with the ability to make meaningful choices.

- Deuteronomy 30:19 (KJV): "I call heaven and earth to record this day against you, that I have set before you life and death, blessing and cursing: therefore choose life, that both thou and thy seed may live:"

The Nature of Temptation

The narrative highlights the subtlety of temptation and the ways in which it can distort truth and appeal to human desires.

- James 1:14-15 (KJV): "But every man is tempted, when he is drawn away of his own lust, and enticed. Then when lust hath conceived, it bringeth forth sin: and sin, when it is finished, bringeth forth death."

The Consequences of Disobedience

The fall illustrates the severe consequences of disobedience, not only for individuals but for all of creation. It underscores the gravity of sin and the disruption it brings to the created order.

- Romans 5:12 (KJV): "Wherefore, as by one man sin entered into the world, and death by sin; and so death passed upon all men, for that all have sinned:"

God's Redemptive Plan

Despite the fall, the narrative sets the stage for God's redemptive plan. The promise of a redeemer foreshadows the coming of Jesus Christ, who will ultimately restore what was lost.

- Genesis 3:15 (KJV): "And I will put enmity between thee and the woman, and between thy seed and her seed; it shall bruise thy head, and thou shalt bruise his heel."

Expository Study with Strong's Concordance

Knowledge ("דַּעַת" daath)

The Hebrew word "דַּעַת" (daath), Strong's H1847, refers to knowledge, understanding, and perception. In the context of the tree, it implies a profound awareness of good and evil that comes with moral responsibility.

- Proverbs 1:7 (KJV): "The fear of the LORD is the beginning of knowledge: but fools despise wisdom and instruction."

Good ("טוֹב" tov) and Evil ("רָע" ra)

The Hebrew words for good, "טוֹב" (tov), Strong's H2896, and evil, "רָע" (ra), Strong's H7451, encapsulate the moral dimensions that humans become aware of through their disobedience.

- Genesis 3:22 (KJV): "And the LORD God said, Behold, the man is become as one of us, to know good and evil: and now, lest he put forth his hand, and take also of the tree of life, and eat, and live for ever:"

Practical Reflections

Moral Choices Today

The story of the tree of knowledge of good and evil serves as a reminder of the importance of making moral choices and the consequences that follow.

- Proverbs 3:5-6 (KJV): "Trust in the LORD with all thine heart; and lean not unto thine own understanding. In all thy ways acknowledge him, and he shall direct thy paths."

Dependence on God's Wisdom

Humans are called to rely on God's wisdom rather than their own understanding. The narrative encourages humility and trust in God's guidance.

- James 1:5 (KJV): "If any of you lack wisdom, let him ask of God, that giveth to all men liberally, and upbraideth not; and it shall be given him."

Hope in Redemption

The fall does not have the final word. The promise of redemption through Jesus Christ offers hope and restoration.

- Romans 5:18-19 (KJV): "Therefore as by the offence of one judgment came upon all men to condemnation; even so by the righteousness of one the free gift came upon all men unto justification of life. For as by one man's disobedience many were made sinners, so by the obedience of one shall many be made righteous."

Comprehensive Commentary

Interpreting the Tree's Significance

The tree of knowledge of good and evil is a multifaceted symbol that encapsulates themes of free will, moral responsibility, temptation, and the consequences of sin. Its presence in the Garden of Eden is integral to understanding the human condition and God's redemptive plan.

Balancing God's Sovereignty and Human Free Will

The narrative highlights the tension between God's sovereignty and human free will. While God establishes boundaries, humans are given the freedom to choose, underscoring the dynamic relationship between divine authority and human agency.

The Role of Obedience in Relationship with God

Obedience is central to maintaining a right relationship with God. The tree serves as a tangible reminder of the need to trust and obey God's commands.

The tree of knowledge of good and evil is a profound and complex element in the Genesis narrative. It serves as a focal point for understanding human free will, moral responsibility, and the consequences of disobedience. Despite the fall, the story sets the stage for God's redemptive work through Jesus Christ, offering hope and restoration. This chapter has explored the biblical foundations, theological implications, and practical reflections on the tree of knowledge of good and evil, providing a comprehensive understanding of its significance in the biblical narrative.

CHAPTER 04

THE GIFT OF FREE WILL

Free will is a fundamental aspect of human existence, deeply embedded in the fabric of theological, philosophical, and ethical discussions. It is the capacity to make choices that are not determined by prior causes or divine intervention. This chapter explores the definition and importance of free will, its biblical foundations, and its significance in the broader context of human life and relationship with God.

Definition of Free Will

Conceptual Understanding

Free will refers to the ability of individuals to make choices that are not predetermined by external factors or divine predestination. It encompasses the capacity for self-determination and moral responsibility.

Philosophical Perspectives

Philosophers have long debated the nature of free will, with various schools of thought offering differing views:

- Libertarian Free Will: Asserts that humans have genuine freedom to choose among alternatives, and these choices are not determined by prior events.

- Compatibilism: Suggests that free will is compatible with determinism, where human choices are free as long as they are not coerced.

- Determinism: Argues that all events, including human actions, are determined by preceding causes.

Biblical Definition

In the biblical context, free will is seen as a gift from God, enabling humans to choose between obedience and disobedience, good and evil.

- Deuteronomy 30:19 (KJV): "I call heaven and earth to record this day against you, that I have set before you life and death, blessing and cursing: therefore choose life, that both thou and thy seed may live."

Biblical Foundations of Free Will

Creation and Free Will

The concept of free will is introduced in the creation narrative. Adam and Eve were given the freedom to choose whether to obey God's command regarding the tree of knowledge of good and evil.

- Genesis 2:16-17 (KJV): "And the LORD God commanded the man, saying, Of every tree of the garden thou mayest freely eat: But of the tree of the knowledge of good and evil, thou shalt not eat of it: for in the day that thou eatest thereof thou shalt surely die."

The Fall and the Exercise of Free Will

The exercise of free will is vividly illustrated in the account of the fall. Adam and Eve's choice to eat the forbidden fruit exemplifies the human capacity to choose disobedience.

- Genesis 3:6 (KJV): "And when the woman saw that the tree was good for food, and that it was pleasant to the eyes, and a tree to be desired to make one wise, she took of the fruit thereof, and did eat, and gave also unto her husband with her; and he did eat."

Moral Responsibility and Accountability

The Bible underscores the importance of free will in moral responsibility. Humans are accountable for their choices, and this accountability is a recurring theme throughout Scripture.

- Joshua 24:15 (KJV): "And if it seem evil unto you to serve the LORD, choose you this day whom ye will serve; whether the gods which your fathers served that were on the other side of the flood, or the gods of the Amorites, in whose land ye dwell: but as for me and my house, we will serve the LORD."

The Importance of Free Will

Relational Aspect with God

Free will is crucial for a genuine relationship with God. Love and obedience must be freely chosen to be meaningful.

- John 14:15 (KJV): "If ye love me, keep my commandments."

Moral Growth and Development

Free will allows for moral growth and the development of virtues. Through making choices, individuals grow in character and maturity.

- James 1:12 (KJV): "Blessed is the man that endureth temptation: for when he is tried, he shall receive the crown of life, which the Lord hath promised to them that love him."

The Possibility of Redemption

The concept of free will is essential to the Christian understanding of redemption. Salvation is offered to all, but individuals must freely choose to accept it.

- Revelation 22:17 (KJV): "And the Spirit and the bride say, Come. And let him that heareth say, Come. And let him that is athirst come. And whosoever will, let him take the water of life freely."

Human Dignity and Value

Free will affirms human dignity and value. It acknowledges individuals as autonomous beings capable of making meaningful decisions.

- Psalm 8:4-5 (KJV): "What is man, that thou art mindful of him? and the son of man, that thou visitest him? For thou hast made him a little lower than the angels, and hast crowned him with glory and honour."

Expository Study with Strong's Concordance

Choose ("בָּחַר" bachar)

The Hebrew word "בָּחַר" (bachar), Strong's H977, means to choose, select, or elect. This term emphasizes the act of making a choice based on preference and decision.

- Deuteronomy 30:19 (KJV): "I call heaven and earth to record this day against you, that I have set before you life and death, blessing and cursing: therefore choose life, that both thou and thy seed may live."

Will ("θέλω" thelo)

The Greek word "θέλω" (thelo), Strong's G2309, denotes to will, wish, desire, or intend. It reflects the inclination or determination to make a particular choice.

- Revelation 22:17 (KJV): "And the Spirit and the bride say, Come. And let him that heareth say, Come. And let him that is athirst come. And whosoever will, let him take the water of life freely."

Theological Implications of Free Will

The Nature of Sin and Responsibility

Free will is integral to understanding sin and human responsibility. Sin is not merely an inherited condition but also involves active choices to disobey God.

- Romans 3:23 (KJV): "For all have sinned, and come short of the glory of God."

God's Sovereignty and Human Free Will

The relationship between God's sovereignty and human free will is a profound theological mystery. While God is sovereign, He allows humans the freedom to choose, which is necessary for genuine love and moral responsibility.

- Philippians 2:12-13 (KJV): "Wherefore, my beloved, as ye have always obeyed, not as in my presence only, but now much more in my absence, work out your own salvation with fear and trembling. For it is God which worketh in you both to will and to do of his good pleasure."

The Role of Grace

Grace plays a crucial role in enabling and guiding free will. God's grace empowers individuals to make righteous choices and seek Him earnestly.

- Ephesians 2:8-9 (KJV): "For by grace are ye saved through faith; and that not of yourselves: it is the gift of God: Not of works, lest any man should boast."

Practical Reflections on Free Will

Making Moral Choices

Free will calls individuals to make moral choices that align with God's will. This involves daily decisions that reflect integrity, compassion, and faithfulness.

- Micah 6:8 (KJV): "He hath shewed thee, O man, what is good; and what doth the LORD require of thee, but to do justly, and to love mercy, and to walk humbly with thy God?"

Living Responsibly

Acknowledging the gift of free will encourages living responsibly, recognizing the impact of one's choices on oneself, others, and the environment.

- Galatians 6:7-8 (KJV): "Be not deceived; God is not mocked: for whatsoever a man soweth, that shall he also reap.

For he that soweth to his flesh shall of the flesh reap corruption; but he that soweth to the Spirit shall of the Spirit reap life everlasting."

Seeking God's Guidance

Free will must be exercised with wisdom and discernment. Seeking God's guidance through prayer and Scripture helps in making choices that honor Him.

- James 1:5 (KJV): "If any of you lack wisdom, let him ask of God, that giveth to all men liberally, and upbraideth not; and it shall be given him."

Comprehensive Commentary

Interpreting Free Will

Free will is not just the ability to choose but the capacity to make choices that reflect God's image and purposes. It is a dynamic interplay of freedom, responsibility, and grace.

Balancing Freedom and Responsibility

While free will grants freedom, it also entails responsibility. Every choice carries consequences, reinforcing the importance of thoughtful and deliberate decision-making.

The Role of Community

Free will is exercised within the context of community. Accountability and mutual encouragement help individuals make choices that contribute to the common good.

- Hebrews 10:24-25 (KJV): "And let us consider one another to provoke unto love and to good works: Not forsaking the assembling of ourselves together, as the manner of some is; but exhorting one another: and so much the more, as ye see the day approaching."

The gift of free will is a profound aspect of human existence, reflecting the image of God and enabling genuine relationship, moral growth, and meaningful choices. This chapter has explored the definition and importance of free will, its biblical foundations, and its theological and practical implications. Understanding and exercising free will responsibly is essential for living a life that honors God and contributes to the flourishing of creation.

Biblical Examples of Free Will in Action

Free will is a central theme in the Bible, reflecting humanity's capacity to make choices that shape their destiny and relationship with God. The Scriptures provide numerous examples of individuals exercising their free will, for better or worse. This chapter explores key biblical narratives that illustrate free will in action, highlighting the consequences of these choices and the lessons they offer.

Adam and Eve: The Choice in Eden

The Decision

Adam and Eve's choice to eat from the tree of the knowledge of good and evil is one of the most profound examples of free will in action. Their decision to disobey God's command had far-reaching consequences.

- Genesis 3:1-6 (KJV): "Now the serpent was more subtil than any beast of the field which the LORD God had made. And he said unto the woman, Yea, hath God said, Ye shall not eat of every tree of the garden? And the woman said unto the serpent, We may eat of the fruit of the trees of the garden: But of the fruit of the tree which is in the midst of the garden, God hath said, Ye shall not eat of it, neither shall ye touch it, lest ye die. And the serpent said unto the woman, Ye shall not surely die: For God doth know that in the day ye eat thereof, then your eyes shall be opened, and ye shall be as gods, knowing good and evil. And when the woman saw that the tree was good for food, and that it was pleasant to the eyes, and a tree to be desired to make one wise, she took of the fruit thereof, and did eat, and gave also unto her husband with her; and he did eat."

The Consequences

Their choice introduced sin and death into the world, fundamentally altering human existence and the relationship between God and humanity.

- Genesis 3:16-19 (KJV): "Unto the woman he said, I will greatly multiply thy sorrow and thy conception; in sorrow thou shalt bring forth children; and thy desire shall be to thy husband, and he shall rule over thee. And unto Adam he said, Because thou hast hearkened unto the voice of thy wife, and hast eaten of the tree, of which I commanded thee, saying, Thou shalt not eat of it: cursed is the ground for thy sake; in sorrow shalt thou eat of it all the days of thy life; Thorns also and thistles shall it bring forth to thee; and thou shalt eat the herb of the field; In the sweat of thy face shalt thou eat bread, till thou return unto the ground; for out of it wast thou taken: for dust thou art, and unto dust shalt thou return."

Lessons Learned

The story of Adam and Eve underscores the importance of obedience to God and the far-reaching impact of our choices. It also highlights the role of temptation and the need for discernment.

Cain and Abel: The Choice of Sacrifice

The Decision

Cain and Abel, the sons of Adam and Eve, made different choices regarding their sacrifices to God. Abel offered a more acceptable sacrifice, while Cain's was rejected, leading to jealousy and murder.

- Genesis 4:3-8 (KJV): "And in process of time it came to pass, that Cain brought of the fruit of the ground an offering unto the LORD. And Abel, he also brought of the firstlings of his flock and of the fat thereof. And the LORD had respect unto Abel and to his offering: But unto Cain and to his offering he had not respect. And Cain was very wroth, and his countenance fell. And the LORD said unto Cain, Why art thou wroth? and why is thy countenance fallen? If thou doest well, shalt thou not be accepted? and if thou doest not well, sin lieth at the door. And unto thee shall be his desire, and thou shalt rule over him. And Cain talked with Abel his brother: and it came to pass, when they were in the field, that Cain rose up against Abel his brother, and slew him."

The Consequences

Cain's choice to kill Abel led to his banishment and a life of wandering, illustrating the destructive power of unchecked anger and jealousy.

- Genesis 4:11-12 (KJV): "And now art thou cursed from the earth, which hath opened her mouth to receive thy brother's blood from thy hand; When thou tillest the ground, it shall not henceforth yield unto thee her strength; a fugitive and a vagabond shalt thou be in the earth."

Lessons Learned

The story of Cain and Abel teaches about the consequences of our choices, the importance of righteous living, and the dangers of allowing negative emotions to control our actions.

Abraham: The Choice of Faith

The Decision

Abraham's willingness to leave his homeland and follow God's call is a powerful example of free will exercised in faith.

- Genesis 12:1-4 (KJV): "Now the LORD had said unto Abram, Get thee out of thy country, and from thy kindred, and from thy father's house, unto a land that I will shew thee: And I will make of thee a great nation, and I will bless thee, and make thy name great; and thou shalt be a blessing: And I will bless them that bless thee, and curse him that curseth thee: and in thee shall all families of the earth be blessed. So Abram departed, as the LORD had spoken unto him; and Lot went with him: and Abram was seventy and five years old when he departed out of Haran."

The Consequences

Abraham's choice to obey God's call set the foundation for the nation of Israel and God's redemptive plan for humanity.

- Genesis 22:15-18 (KJV): "And the angel of the LORD called unto Abraham out of heaven the second time, And said, By myself have I sworn, saith the LORD, for because thou hast done this thing, and hast not withheld thy son, thine only son: That in blessing I will bless thee, and in multiplying I will multiply thy seed as the stars of the heaven, and as the sand which is upon the sea shore; and thy seed shall possess the gate of his enemies; And in thy seed shall all the nations of the earth be blessed; because thou hast obeyed my voice."

Lessons Learned

Abraham's story highlights the importance of faith and trust in God's promises. It shows how free will can be aligned with divine purposes, leading to blessings and fulfillment of God's plan.

Moses: The Choice of Leadership

The Decision

Moses' choice to confront Pharaoh and lead the Israelites out of Egypt demonstrates courage and obedience to God's call.

- Exodus 3:10-12 (KJV): "Come now therefore, and I will send thee unto Pharaoh, that thou mayest bring forth my people the children of Israel out of Egypt. And Moses said unto God, Who am I, that I should go unto Pharaoh, and that

I should bring forth the children of Israel out of Egypt? And he said, Certainly I will be with thee; and this shall be a token unto thee, that I have sent thee: When thou hast brought forth the people out of Egypt, ye shall serve God upon this mountain."

The Consequences

Moses' choice led to the deliverance of the Israelites and the establishment of the covenant at Sinai, shaping the identity and destiny of the nation.

- Exodus 19:5-6 (KJV): "Now therefore, if ye will obey my voice indeed, and keep my covenant, then ye shall be a peculiar treasure unto me above all people: for all the earth is mine: And ye shall be unto me a kingdom of priests, and an holy nation. These are the words which thou shalt speak unto the children of Israel."

Lessons Learned

The story of Moses illustrates the impact of faithful leadership and the importance of responding to God's call despite personal inadequacies and fears.

David: The Choice of Repentance

The Decision

King David's life provides several examples of free will in action, notably his sin with Bathsheba and his subsequent repentance.

- 2 Samuel 11:2-4 (KJV): "And it came to pass in an eveningtide, that David arose from off his bed, and walked upon the roof of the king's house: and from the roof he saw a woman washing herself; and the woman was very beautiful to look upon. And David sent and enquired after the woman. And one said, Is not this Bathsheba, the daughter of Eliam, the wife of Uriah the Hittite? And David sent messengers, and took her; and she came in unto him, and he lay with her; for she was purified from her uncleanness: and she returned unto her house."

The Consequences

David's sin brought severe consequences, including the death of the child born from the affair and ongoing turmoil in his family. However, his heartfelt repentance restored his relationship with God.

- Psalm 51:1-4 (KJV): "Have mercy upon me, O God, according to thy lovingkindness: according unto the multitude of thy tender mercies blot out my transgressions. Wash me thoroughly from mine iniquity, and cleanse me from my sin. For I acknowledge my transgressions: and my sin is ever before me. Against thee, thee only, have I sinned, and done this evil in thy sight: that thou mightest be justified when thou speakest, and be clear when thou judgest."

Lessons Learned

David's story emphasizes the reality of sin and its consequences but also the power of genuine repentance and God's readiness to forgive.

Jesus: The Choice of Sacrifice

The Decision

Jesus Christ's choice to submit to the Father's will and sacrifice Himself for humanity's sins is the ultimate example of free will aligned with divine purpose.

- Matthew 26:39 (KJV): "And he went a little farther, and fell on his face, and prayed, saying, O my Father, if it be possible, let this cup pass from me: nevertheless not as I will, but as thou wilt."

The Consequences

Jesus' sacrificial choice brought redemption and salvation to humanity, fulfilling God's plan for reconciliation and eternal life.

- Philippians 2:8 (KJV): "And being found in fashion as a man, he humbled himself, and became obedient unto death, even the death of the cross."

Lessons Learned

Jesus' example teaches the profound significance of obedience, sacrifice, and aligning one's will with God's will. It highlights the transformative power of selfless love and devotion.

Practical Reflections on Free Will in Action

Everyday Choices

The biblical examples of free will in action remind us that our everyday choices matter. They shape our character, impact our relationships, and reflect our values and faith.

- Galatians 6:7-8 (KJV): "Be not deceived; God is not mocked: for whatsoever a man soweth, that shall he also reap. For he that soweth to his flesh shall of the flesh reap corruption; but he that soweth to the Spirit shall of the Spirit reap life everlasting."

Seeking God's Guidance

Exercising free will responsibly requires seeking God's guidance through prayer, Scripture, and wise counsel.

- James 1:5 (KJV): "If any of you lack wisdom, let him ask of God, that giveth to all men liberally, and upbraideth not; and it shall be given him."

Embracing Accountability

Understanding the consequences of our choices calls for a life of accountability, where we take responsibility for our actions and their impact on others.

- Romans 14:12 (KJV): "So then every one of us shall give account of himself to God."

Comprehensive Commentary

Interpreting Free Will in Biblical Context

The biblical narratives illustrate that free will is integral to human existence. It is a gift that allows for genuine relationships, moral growth, and participation in God's redemptive work.

Balancing Free Will and Divine Sovereignty

These stories also highlight the dynamic interplay between human free will and divine sovereignty. God's purposes ultimately prevail, but He works through and respects human choices.

The Role of Community in Exercising Free Will

Exercising free will is not an isolated endeavor but occurs within the context of community. Mutual encouragement and accountability help individuals make choices that honor God and benefit others.

The biblical examples of free will in action provide valuable insights into the nature and significance of human choice. From Adam and Eve's disobedience to Jesus' sacrificial obedience, these stories reveal the profound impact of our decisions and the importance of aligning our will with God's purposes. Understanding and exercising free will responsibly is essential for living a life that honors God and contributes to the flourishing of creation.

Theological Implications of Free Will

Free will is a fundamental concept that has profound theological implications. It affects our understanding of human nature, sin, redemption, divine sovereignty, and moral responsibility. This chapter explores the theological implications of free will, examining how it shapes key doctrines and our relationship with God.

Human Nature and Free Will

Image of God (Imago Dei)

Free will is a crucial aspect of being created in the image of God. It reflects God's nature as a free and sovereign being and endows humans with the capacity to make choices.

- Genesis 1:26-27 (KJV): "And God said, Let us make man in our image, after our likeness: and let them have dominion over the fish of the sea, and over the fowl of the air, and over the cattle, and over all the earth, and over every creeping thing that creepeth upon the earth. So God created man in his own image, in the image of God created he him; male and female created he them."

Dignity and Responsibility

The gift of free will imparts dignity to human beings, recognizing them as moral agents capable of making meaningful decisions. It also carries the weight of responsibility for those decisions.

- Psalm 8:4-6 (KJV): "What is man, that thou art mindful of him? and the son of man, that thou visitest him? For thou hast made him a little lower than the angels, and hast crowned him with glory and honour. Thou madest him to have dominion over the works of thy hands; thou hast put all things under his feet."

Sin and Free Will

The Origin of Sin

The exercise of free will is central to the biblical account of the fall. Adam and Eve's choice to disobey God introduced sin into the world.

- Genesis 3:6 (KJV): "And when the woman saw that the tree was good for food, and that it was pleasant to the eyes, and a tree to be desired to make one wise, she took of the fruit thereof, and did eat, and gave also unto her husband with her; and he did eat."

Moral Accountability

Free will means that individuals are morally accountable for their actions. Sin is not just an inherited condition but also involves active choices to disobey God.

- Romans 3:23 (KJV): "For all have sinned, and come short of the glory of God."

Consequences of Sin

The choices made through free will have consequences, both temporal and eternal. The Bible teaches that sin leads to spiritual death and separation from God.

- Romans 6:23 (KJV): "For the wages of sin is death; but the gift of God is eternal life through Jesus Christ our Lord."

Redemption and Free Will

God's Offer of Salvation

The concept of free will is essential to the Christian understanding of redemption. Salvation is offered to all, but individuals must freely choose to accept it.

- Revelation 22:17 (KJV): "And the Spirit and the bride say, Come. And let him that heareth say, Come. And let him that is athirst come. And whosoever will, let him take the water of life freely."

Grace and Free Will

Grace plays a crucial role in enabling and guiding free will. God's grace empowers individuals to make righteous choices and seek Him earnestly.

- Ephesians 2:8-9 (KJV): "For by grace are ye saved through faith; and that not of yourselves: it is the gift of God: Not of works, lest any man should boast."

Cooperation with Divine Will

Redemption involves a cooperative relationship between human free will and divine grace. Believers are called to work out their salvation with reverence, recognizing that God is at work within them.

- Philippians 2:12-13 (KJV): "Wherefore, my beloved, as ye have always obeyed, not as in my presence only, but now much more in my absence, work out your own salvation with fear and trembling. For it is God which worketh in you both to will and to do of his good pleasure."

Divine Sovereignty and Free Will

God's Sovereignty

God is sovereign over all creation, yet He allows humans to exercise free will. This dynamic relationship underscores God's ultimate authority and human responsibility.

- Isaiah 46:9-10 (KJV): "Remember the former things of old: for I am God, and there is none else; I am God, and there is none like me, Declaring the end from the beginning, and from ancient times the things that are not yet done, saying, My counsel shall stand, and I will do all my pleasure."

Compatibilism

Some theological perspectives, like compatibilism, suggest that God's sovereignty and human free will are compatible. God ordains all that happens, but humans still act freely within God's sovereign plan.

Mystery of Divine Foreknowledge

The relationship between God's foreknowledge and human free will remains a profound mystery. While God knows all future events, human choices are still free and significant.

- Psalm 139:4 (KJV): "For there is not a word in my tongue, but, lo, O LORD, thou knowest it altogether."

Practical Reflections on Free Will

Moral Decision-Making

Free will calls individuals to make moral choices that align with God's will. This involves daily decisions that reflect integrity, compassion, and faithfulness.

- Micah 6:8 (KJV): "He hath shewed thee, O man, what is good; and what doth the LORD require of thee, but to do justly, and to love mercy, and to walk humbly with thy God?"

Living Responsibly

Acknowledging the gift of free will encourages living responsibly, recognizing the impact of one's choices on oneself, others, and the environment.

- Galatians 6:7-8 (KJV): "Be not deceived; God is not mocked: for whatsoever a man soweth, that shall he also reap. For he that soweth to his flesh shall of the flesh reap corruption; but he that soweth to the Spirit shall of the Spirit reap life everlasting."

Seeking God's Guidance

Free will must be exercised with wisdom and discernment. Seeking God's guidance through prayer and Scripture helps in making choices that honor Him.

- James 1:5 (KJV): "If any of you lack wisdom, let him ask of God, that giveth to all men liberally, and upbraideth not; and it shall be given him."

Community and Accountability

Exercising free will is not an isolated endeavor but occurs within the context of community. Mutual encouragement and accountability help individuals make choices that honor God and benefit others.

- Hebrews 10:24-25 (KJV): "And let us consider one another to provoke unto love and to good works: Not forsaking the assembling of ourselves together, as the manner of some is; but exhorting one another: and so much the more, as ye see the day approaching."

Expository Study with Strong's Concordance

Choose ("בָּחַר" bachar)

The Hebrew word "בָּחַר" (bachar), Strong's H977, means to choose, select, or elect. This term emphasizes the act of making a choice based on preference and decision.

- Deuteronomy 30:19 (KJV): "I call heaven and earth to record this day against you, that I have set before you life and death, blessing and cursing: therefore choose life, that both thou and thy seed may live."

Will ("θέλω" thelo)

The Greek word "θέλω" (thelo), Strong's G2309, denotes to will, wish, desire, or intend. It reflects the inclination or determination to make a particular choice.

- Revelation 22:17 (KJV): "And the Spirit and the bride say, Come. And let him that heareth say, Come. And let him that is athirst come. And whosoever will, let him take the water of life freely."

Comprehensive Commentary

Interpreting Free Will in Theological Context

Free will is integral to understanding key theological concepts such as sin, redemption, and divine sovereignty. It underscores the relational aspect of humanity's interaction with God, highlighting the importance of voluntary obedience and love.

Balancing Free Will and Divine Sovereignty

The balance between free will and divine sovereignty remains a theological mystery. Recognizing this balance helps believers appreciate the dynamic relationship between human responsibility and God's overarching plan.

The Role of Grace in Exercising Free Will

Grace is essential for the proper exercise of free will. It empowers and guides individuals to make choices that align with God's will and purposes.

Practical Theology

Understanding the theological implications of free will has practical applications. It informs ethical decision-making, encourages personal responsibility, and fosters a deeper reliance on God's guidance and grace.

The theological implications of free will are vast and profound, affecting our understanding of human nature, sin, redemption, and divine sovereignty. Free will endows humans with dignity and responsibility, shaping their moral and spiritual journey. By exploring the biblical foundations and theological significance of free will, believers can gain a deeper appreciation of this gift and its impact on their relationship with God and the world. This chapter has provided a comprehensive exploration of the theological implications of free will, laying the groundwork for further discussions on its role in the Christian life and doctrine.

Do Angels Have Free Will?

The question of whether angels possess free will is a significant theological inquiry with implications for understanding the nature of angels, the fall of Satan, and the broader framework of free will in creation. This chapter explores biblical and theological perspectives on angelic free will, examining scriptural evidence, theological implications, and the consequences of angelic choices.

Biblical Evidence for Angelic Free Will

The Fall of Satan and His Angels

The fall of Satan and the rebellion of other angels provide the most compelling evidence that angels possess free will. Satan, originally an archangel, chose to rebel against God, leading to his fall.

- Isaiah 14:12-15 (KJV): "How art thou fallen from heaven, O Lucifer, son of the morning! how art thou cut down to the ground, which didst weaken the nations! For thou hast said in thine heart, I will ascend into heaven, I will exalt my throne above the stars of God: I will sit also upon the mount of the congregation, in the sides of the north: I will ascend above the heights of the clouds; I will be like the most High. Yet thou shalt be brought down to hell, to the sides of the pit."

- Ezekiel 28:12-17 (KJV): "Son of man, take up a lamentation upon the king of Tyrus, and say unto him, Thus saith the Lord GOD; Thou sealest up the sum, full of wisdom, and perfect in beauty. Thou hast been in Eden the garden of God; every precious stone was thy covering...Thou wast perfect in thy ways from the day that thou wast created, till iniquity was found in thee. By the multitude of thy merchandise they have filled the midst of thee with violence, and thou hast sinned: therefore I will cast thee as profane out of the mountain of God: and I will destroy thee, O covering cherub, from the midst of the stones of fire."

- Revelation 12:7-9 (KJV): "And there was war in heaven: Michael and his angels fought against the dragon; and the dragon fought and his angels, And prevailed not; neither was their place found any more in heaven. And the great dragon was cast out, that old serpent, called the Devil, and Satan, which deceiveth the whole world: he was cast out into the earth, and his angels were cast out with him."

The Obedience of Holy Angels

Conversely, holy angels are depicted as choosing to obey and serve God, reinforcing the notion that they act out of free will rather than compulsion.

- Psalm 103:20 (KJV): "Bless the LORD, ye his angels, that excel in strength, that do his commandments, hearkening unto the voice of his word."

- Hebrews 1:14 (KJV): "Are they not all ministering spirits, sent forth to minister for them who shall be heirs of salvation?"

Theological Implications of Angelic Free Will

Moral Responsibility

If angels possess free will, they are morally responsible for their actions. This responsibility is evident in the punishment of fallen angels and the continued service of holy angels.

- 2 Peter 2:4 (KJV): "For if God spared not the angels that sinned, but cast them down to hell, and delivered them into chains of darkness, to be reserved unto judgment."

Nature of Sin and Rebellion

The rebellion of Satan and his angels illustrates that free will includes the potential for sin and rebellion. Their choice to oppose God underscores the reality of moral agency among angelic beings.

- Jude 1:6 (KJV): "And the angels which kept not their first estate, but left their own habitation, he hath reserved in everlasting chains under darkness unto the judgment of the great day."

Divine Justice and Mercy

The exercise of free will by angels highlights the justice of God in punishing rebellion and His mercy in upholding the faithful service of holy angels.

- Matthew 25:41 (KJV): "Then shall he say also unto them on the left hand, Depart from me, ye cursed, into everlasting fire, prepared for the devil and his angels."

Consequences of Angelic Choices

Impact on Human History

The choices made by angels, both holy and fallen, have significant implications for human history. Satan's rebellion and subsequent actions have led to widespread spiritual warfare and temptation for humanity.

- Ephesians 6:12 (KJV): "For we wrestle not against flesh and blood, but against principalities, against powers, against the rulers of the darkness of this world, against spiritual wickedness in high places."

Role in Salvation History

Holy angels play a vital role in the unfolding of God's redemptive plan, ministering to believers and executing divine judgment.

- Luke 1:26-28 (KJV): "And in the sixth month the angel Gabriel was sent from God unto a city of Galilee, named Nazareth, To a virgin espoused to a man whose name was Joseph, of the house of David; and the virgin's name was Mary. And the angel came in unto her, and said, Hail, thou that art highly favoured, the Lord is with thee: blessed art thou among women."

- Matthew 28:2-5 (KJV): "And, behold, there was a great earthquake: for the angel of the Lord descended from heaven, and came and rolled back the stone from the door, and sat upon it. His countenance was like lightning, and his raiment white as snow: And for fear of him the keepers did shake, and became as dead men. And the angel answered and said unto the women, Fear not ye: for I know that ye seek Jesus, which was crucified."

Eternal Destinies

The eternal destinies of angels are determined by their choices. Fallen angels face eternal punishment, while holy angels dwell eternally in God's presence.

- Revelation 20:10 (KJV): "And the devil that deceived them was cast into the lake of fire and brimstone, where the beast and the false prophet are, and shall be tormented day and night for ever and ever."

Expository Study with Strong's Concordance

Angel ("ἄγγελος" aggelos)

The Greek word "ἄγγελος" (aggelos), Strong's G32, means messenger. It is used to describe both human and divine messengers, but primarily refers to celestial beings who serve as God's messengers.

- Hebrews 1:14 (KJV): "Are they not all ministering spirits, sent forth to minister for them who shall be heirs of salvation?"

Will ("θέλω" thelo)

The Greek word "θέλω" (thelo), Strong's G2309, denotes to will, wish, desire, or intend. It reflects the inclination or determination to make a particular choice, applicable to both humans and angels.

- Revelation 12:7-8 (KJV): "And there was war in heaven: Michael and his angels fought against the dragon; and the dragon fought and his angels, And prevailed not; neither was their place found any more in heaven."

Practical Reflections on Angelic Free Will

Human Choices and Spiritual Warfare

Understanding that angels possess free will and can choose rebellion highlights the reality of spiritual warfare. Believers must remain vigilant and discerning, aware of the spiritual battles that influence their lives.

- 1 Peter 5:8 (KJV): "Be sober, be vigilant; because your adversary the devil, as a roaring lion, walketh about, seeking whom he may devour."

Role of Angels in Daily Life

Holy angels continue to serve and assist believers. Recognizing their role can provide comfort and encouragement in times of difficulty.

- Psalm 91:11-12 (KJV): "For he shall give his angels charge over thee, to keep thee in all thy ways. They shall bear thee up in their hands, lest thou dash thy foot against a stone."

Reflecting on God's Sovereignty

The existence of free will among angels reinforces the sovereignty and justice of God. It demonstrates that God's creation includes beings with the capacity to choose, underscoring the importance of voluntary obedience and worship.

- Romans 11:33-34 (KJV): "O the depth of the riches both of the wisdom and knowledge of God! how unsearchable are his judgments, and his ways past finding out! For who hath known the mind of the Lord? or who hath been his counsellor?"

Comprehensive Commentary

Interpreting Angelic Free Will

The concept of free will among angels aligns with the broader biblical narrative of moral agency and responsibility. It highlights the complex and dynamic nature of God's creation, where even celestial beings make significant choices.

Balancing Free Will and Divine Sovereignty

The coexistence of angelic free will and divine sovereignty reflects a profound theological balance. God's ultimate plan and purposes prevail, yet He allows angels to exercise free will, resulting in meaningful and consequential choices.

The Role of Angels in God's Plan

Angels play a crucial role in God's redemptive plan, serving as messengers, protectors, and executors of divine will. Their free will underscores their voluntary participation in this divine mission.

The question of whether angels possess free will is answered affirmatively through biblical evidence and theological reflection. Angels, like humans, have the capacity to make choices, resulting in significant consequences for themselves and humanity. Understanding angelic free will enriches our comprehension of the spiritual realm, the nature of sin and rebellion, and the broader framework of moral agency in God's creation. This chapter has provided a comprehensive exploration of angelic free will, its implications, and practical reflections for believers.

CHAPTER 05

THE FALL OF HUMANITY

The Story of Adam and Eve and the Introduction of Sin

The story of Adam and Eve in the Garden of Eden is foundational to understanding the human condition, the introduction of sin, and the necessity of redemption. This chapter explores the biblical narrative of the fall, its theological implications, and the profound impact it has on humanity and creation.

The Creation of Adam and Eve

The Formation of Adam

Adam, the first human, was created by God from the dust of the ground and given life through God's breath.

- Genesis 2:7 (KJV): "And the LORD God formed man of the dust of the ground, and breathed into his nostrils the breath of life; and man became a living soul."

The Creation of Eve

Eve was created from one of Adam's ribs to be his companion, establishing the first human relationship.

- Genesis 2:21-23 (KJV): "And the LORD God caused a deep sleep to fall upon Adam, and he slept: and he took one of his ribs, and closed up the flesh instead thereof; And the rib, which the LORD God had taken from man, made he a woman, and brought her unto the man. And Adam said, This is now bone of my bones, and flesh of my flesh: she shall be called Woman, because she was taken out of Man."

The Garden of Eden

God placed Adam and Eve in the Garden of Eden, a paradise filled with every kind of tree and plant, including the tree of life and the tree of the knowledge of good and evil.

- Genesis 2:8-9 (KJV): "And the LORD God planted a garden eastward in Eden; and there he put the man whom he had formed. And out of the ground made the LORD God to grow every tree that is pleasant to the sight, and good for food; the tree of life also in the midst of the garden, and the tree of knowledge of good and evil."

The Command and the Temptation

God's Command

God gave Adam and Eve the freedom to eat from any tree in the garden except the tree of the knowledge of good and evil, warning them that eating its fruit would result in death.

- Genesis 2:16-17 (KJV): "And the LORD God commanded the man, saying, Of every tree of the garden thou mayest freely eat: But of the tree of the knowledge of good and evil, thou shalt not eat of it: for in the day that thou eatest thereof thou shalt surely die."

The Serpent's Deception

The serpent, more cunning than any other creature, tempted Eve by questioning God's command and suggesting that eating the fruit would make them like God, knowing good and evil.

- Genesis 3:1-5 (KJV): "Now the serpent was more subtil than any beast of the field which the LORD God had made. And he said unto the woman, Yea, hath God said, Ye shall not eat of every tree of the garden? And the woman said unto the serpent, We may eat of the fruit of the trees of the garden: But of the fruit of the tree which is in the midst of the garden, God hath said, Ye shall not eat of it, neither shall ye touch it, lest ye die. And the serpent said unto the woman, Ye shall not surely die: For God doth know that in the day ye eat thereof, then your eyes shall be opened, and ye shall be as gods, knowing good and evil."

The Choice

Eve, seeing that the fruit was good for food, pleasing to the eye, and desirable for gaining wisdom, ate it and gave some to Adam, who also ate.

- Genesis 3:6 (KJV): "And when the woman saw that the tree was good for food, and that it was pleasant to the eyes, and a tree to be desired to make one wise, she took of the fruit thereof, and did eat, and gave also unto her husband with her; and he did eat."

The Consequences of the Fall

Immediate Consequences

Their disobedience resulted in immediate awareness of their nakedness, leading to shame and fear. They sewed fig leaves together to cover themselves and hid from God.

- Genesis 3:7-10 (KJV): "And the eyes of them both were opened, and they knew that they were naked; and they sewed fig leaves together, and made themselves aprons. And they heard the voice of the LORD God walking in the garden in the cool of the day: and Adam and his wife hid themselves from the presence of the LORD God amongst the trees of the garden. And the LORD God called unto Adam, and said unto him, Where art thou? And he said, I heard thy voice in the garden, and I was afraid, because I was naked; and I hid myself."

God's Judgment

God pronounced judgments on the serpent, Eve, and Adam. The serpent was cursed to crawl on its belly, Eve was given increased pain in childbirth and subjection to her husband, and Adam was condemned to toil and labor for his sustenance until his return to dust.

- Genesis 3:14-19 (KJV): "And the LORD God said unto the serpent, Because thou hast done this, thou art cursed above all cattle, and above every beast of the field; upon thy belly shalt thou go, and dust shalt thou eat all the days of thy life: And I will put enmity between thee and the woman, and between thy seed and her seed; it shall bruise thy head, and thou shalt bruise his heel. Unto the woman he said, I will greatly multiply thy sorrow and thy conception; in sorrow thou shalt bring forth children; and thy desire shall be to thy husband, and he shall rule over thee. And unto Adam he said, Because thou hast hearkened unto the voice of thy wife, and hast eaten of the tree, of which I commanded thee, saying, Thou shalt not eat of it: cursed is the ground for thy sake; in sorrow shalt thou eat of it all the days of thy life; Thorns also and thistles shall it bring forth to thee; and thou shalt eat the herb of the field; In the sweat of thy face shalt thou eat bread, till thou return unto the ground; for out of it wast thou taken: for dust thou art, and unto dust shalt thou return."

Expulsion from Eden

To prevent Adam and Eve from eating from the tree of life and living forever in their fallen state, God expelled them from the Garden of Eden and placed cherubim to guard the way to the tree of life.

- Genesis 3:22-24 (KJV): "And the LORD God said, Behold, the man is become as one of us, to know good and evil: and now, lest he put forth his hand, and take also of the tree of life, and eat, and live for ever: Therefore the LORD God sent him forth from the garden of Eden, to till the ground from whence he was taken. So he drove out the man; and he placed at the east of the garden of Eden Cherubims, and a flaming sword which turned every way, to keep the way of the tree of life."

Theological Implications of the Fall

The Nature of Sin

The fall illustrates that sin is fundamentally about disobedience to God's command and a desire to be autonomous from God's authority.

- Romans 5:19 (KJV): "For as by one man's disobedience many were made sinners, so by the obedience of one shall many be made righteous."

Original Sin

The fall introduced the concept of original sin, the inherited sinful nature passed down from Adam to all humanity. This doctrine explains the universal tendency towards sin and the need for redemption.

- Romans 5:12 (KJV): "Wherefore, as by one man sin entered into the world, and death by sin; and so death passed upon all men, for that all have sinned."

Separation from God

Sin caused a separation between humanity and God, symbolized by Adam and Eve's expulsion from Eden. This separation necessitated a plan of redemption to restore the broken relationship.

- Isaiah 59:2 (KJV): "But your iniquities have separated between you and your God, and your sins have hid his face from you, that he will not hear."

The Protoevangelium

Amidst the pronouncement of judgment, God provided a glimmer of hope through the protoevangelium, the first gospel, which foretold the ultimate defeat of Satan by the seed of the woman.

- Genesis 3:15 (KJV): "And I will put enmity between thee and the woman, and between thy seed and her seed; it shall bruise thy head, and thou shalt bruise his heel."

Expository Study with Strong's Concordance

Sin ("חַטָּאָה" chatta'ah)

The Hebrew word "חַטָּאָה" (chatta'ah), Strong's H2403, means sin or sin offering. It denotes an offense against God's law and a deviation from His will.

- Genesis 4:7 (KJV): "If thou doest well, shalt thou not be accepted? and if thou doest not well, sin lieth at the door. And unto thee shall be his desire, and thou shalt rule over him."

Disobedience ("παρακοή" parakoē)

The Greek word "παρακοή" (parakoē), Strong's G3876, means disobedience or unwillingness to listen. It emphasizes the refusal to heed God's command.

- Romans 5:19 (KJV): "For as by one man's disobedience many were made sinners, so by the obedience of one shall many be made righteous."

Practical Reflections on the Fall

Understanding Human Nature

The fall helps us understand the human propensity towards sin and the struggle between good and evil within each person.

- Romans 7:18-19 (KJV): "For I know that in me (that is, in my flesh,) dwelleth no good thing: for to will is present with me; but how to perform that which is good I find not. For the good that I would I do not: but the evil which I would not, that I do."

The Need for Redemption

Recognizing the impact of the fall highlights the necessity of redemption through Jesus Christ. It underscores humanity's need for a Savior to reconcile us with God.

- John 3:16 (KJV): "For God so loved the world, that he gave his only begotten Son, that whosoever believeth in him should not perish, but have everlasting life."

Living in Grace

Despite the fall, believers are called to live in the grace and redemption offered through Christ, striving to overcome sin and live according to God's will.

- Romans 6:12-14 (KJV): "Let not sin therefore reign in your mortal body, that ye should obey it in the lusts thereof. Neither yield ye your members as instruments of unrighteousness unto sin: but yield yourselves unto God, as those that are alive from the dead, and your members as instruments of righteousness unto God. For sin shall not have dominion over you: for ye are not under the law, but under grace."

Comprehensive Commentary

Interpreting the Fall

The fall of humanity is a pivotal event that explains the origin of sin and its pervasive effects on human life and creation. It sets the stage for understanding the need for divine intervention and redemption.

The Balance of Justice and Mercy

The narrative of the fall demonstrates God's justice in punishing sin and His mercy in providing a promise of redemption. It highlights the dual aspects of God's character as both just and merciful.

The Ongoing Struggle

The fall introduces an ongoing struggle between good and evil, obedience and disobedience, that continues throughout human history. It calls believers to rely on God's strength to overcome sin and live righteously.

The story of Adam and Eve and the introduction of sin is central to the biblical narrative and theological understanding of the human condition. It explains the origin of sin, the separation from God, and the need for redemption. Through the fall, we learn about the consequences of disobedience, the justice and mercy of God, and the promise of redemption through Jesus Christ. This chapter has provided a comprehensive exploration of the fall of humanity, its implications, and its relevance to our understanding of sin and salvation.

Consequences of the Fall: Original Sin and the Presence of Evil

The fall of Adam and Eve in the Garden of Eden had profound and far-reaching consequences for humanity and the entire creation. This chapter explores the doctrine of original sin, the pervasive presence of evil in the world, and the theological and practical implications of these realities. Understanding these consequences is crucial for grasping the depth of human sinfulness and the necessity of redemption through Jesus Christ.

The Doctrine of Original Sin

Definition of Original Sin

Original sin refers to the fallen state of human nature inherited from Adam. It encompasses both the inherited guilt and the corrupted nature that predisposes humans to sin.

- Romans 5:12 (KJV): "Wherefore, as by one man sin entered into the world, and death by sin; and so death passed upon all men, for that all have sinned."

Biblical Foundations

The concept of original sin is rooted in the biblical narrative of Adam's disobedience and its impact on his descendants.

- Psalm 51:5 (KJV): "Behold, I was shapen in iniquity; and in sin did my mother conceive me."

- Ephesians 2:3 (KJV): "Among whom also we all had our conversation in times past in the lusts of our flesh, fulfilling the desires of the flesh and of the mind; and were by nature the children of wrath, even as others."

The Transmission of Original Sin

The doctrine asserts that all humans inherit a sinful nature from Adam, resulting in a propensity to sin and spiritual death.

- 1 Corinthians 15:21-22 (KJV): "For since by man came death, by man came also the resurrection of the dead. For as in Adam all die, even so in Christ shall all be made alive."

The Presence of Evil in the World

The Entry of Evil

The fall introduced moral and natural evil into the world. Moral evil includes human actions that violate God's will, while natural evil encompasses suffering and disasters resulting from the corrupted state of creation.

- Genesis 3:17-19 (KJV): "And unto Adam he said, Because thou hast hearkened unto the voice of thy wife, and hast eaten of the tree, of which I commanded thee, saying, Thou shalt not eat of it: cursed is the ground for thy sake; in sorrow shalt thou eat of it all the days of thy life; Thorns also and thistles shall it bring forth to thee; and thou shalt eat the herb of the field; In the sweat of thy face shalt thou eat bread, till thou return unto the ground; for out of it wast thou taken: for dust thou art, and unto dust shalt thou return."

The Pervasiveness of Evil

Evil pervades every aspect of human existence, affecting individuals, societies, and the natural world. This pervasive presence underscores the fallen nature of creation.

- Romans 8:20-22 (KJV): "For the creature was made subject to vanity, not willingly, but by reason of him who hath subjected the same in hope, Because the creature itself also shall be delivered from the bondage of corruption into the glorious liberty of the children of God. For we know that the whole creation groaneth and travaileth in pain together until now."

Human Suffering and Injustice

The presence of evil manifests in human suffering, injustice, and moral decay. These realities highlight the brokenness of the world and the need for divine intervention.

- Ecclesiastes 4:1 (KJV): "So I returned, and considered all the oppressions that are done under the sun: and behold the tears of such as were oppressed, and they had no comforter; and on the side of their oppressors there was power; but they had no comforter."

Theological Implications of Original Sin and Evil

Human Depravity

Original sin results in human depravity, indicating that every aspect of human nature is tainted by sin. This depravity affects thoughts, actions, and desires.

- Jeremiah 17:9 (KJV): "The heart is deceitful above all things, and desperately wicked: who can know it?"

Separation from God

Sin causes a separation between humanity and God, necessitating a means of reconciliation. This separation is both spiritual and relational.

- Isaiah 59:2 (KJV): "But your iniquities have separated between you and your God, and your sins have hid his face from you, that he will not hear."

The Need for Redemption

The pervasive presence of sin and evil underscores the need for redemption through Jesus Christ. Only through His sacrificial death and resurrection can humanity be reconciled to God.

- Romans 5:18-19 (KJV): "Therefore as by the offence of one judgment came upon all men to condemnation; even so by the righteousness of one the free gift came upon all men unto justification of life. For as by one man's disobedience many were made sinners, so by the obedience of one shall many be made righteous."

Practical Reflections on Original Sin and Evil

Acknowledging Human Sinfulness

Recognizing the reality of original sin calls for humility and repentance. It requires an acknowledgment of personal and collective sinfulness and the need for God's grace.

- 1 John 1:8-9 (KJV): "If we say that we have no sin, we deceive ourselves, and the truth is not in us. If we confess our sins, he is faithful and just to forgive us our sins, and to cleanse us from all unrighteousness."

Living in a Fallen World

Believers are called to navigate the challenges of living in a fallen world. This involves resisting temptation, seeking justice, and offering compassion to those who suffer.

- James 1:27 (KJV): "Pure religion and undefiled before God and the Father is this, To visit the fatherless and widows in their affliction, and to keep himself unspotted from the world."

Hope in Redemption

Despite the pervasive presence of sin and evil, believers hold onto the hope of redemption and restoration through Jesus Christ. This hope encourages perseverance and faithfulness.

- Revelation 21:4 (KJV): "And God shall wipe away all tears from their eyes; and there shall be no more death, neither sorrow, nor crying, neither shall there be any more pain: for the former things are passed away."

Expository Study with Strong's Concordance

Sin ("ἁμαρτία" hamartia)

The Greek word "ἁμαρτία" (hamartia), Strong's G266, means sin, failure, or missing the mark. It denotes actions and attitudes that fall short of God's standards.

- Romans 3:23 (KJV): "For all have sinned, and come short of the glory of God."

Evil ("רָע" ra)

The Hebrew word "רָע" (ra), Strong's H7451, means evil, wickedness, or calamity. It encompasses both moral evil and the resulting suffering.

- Genesis 6:5 (KJV): "And God saw that the wickedness of man was great in the earth, and that every imagination of the thoughts of his heart was only evil continually."

Comprehensive Commentary

Interpreting Original Sin and Evil

The doctrines of original sin and the presence of evil provide a framework for understanding the human condition and the brokenness of the world. They highlight the need for divine intervention and the transformative power of redemption.

Balancing Justice and Mercy

The consequences of the fall demonstrate God's justice in addressing sin and His mercy in providing a means of redemption. This balance is essential for understanding God's character and His plan for humanity.

The Role of Believers

Believers are called to acknowledge their own sinfulness, strive for righteousness, and offer hope and compassion in a world marred by sin and evil. This involves active engagement in justice, mercy, and evangelism.

The consequences of the fall, including original sin and the pervasive presence of evil, profoundly impact human existence and the world. Understanding these realities is crucial for grasping the depth of human sinfulness and the necessity of redemption through Jesus Christ. This chapter has explored the doctrine of original sin, the presence of evil, and their theological and practical implications, providing a comprehensive understanding of the fallen state of humanity and the hope of redemption.

The Relationship Between Free Will and Disobedience

The interplay between free will and disobedience is central to understanding the human condition and the moral landscape within which we operate. The concept of free will allows for genuine moral choices, but it also opens the door to the possibility of disobedience. This chapter explores the relationship between free will and disobedience, examining biblical narratives, theological insights, and practical reflections on how free will can lead to both obedience and disobedience.

The Concept of Free Will

Definition of Free Will

Free will refers to the ability of individuals to make choices that are not determined by prior causes or divine intervention. It encompasses the capacity for self-determination and moral responsibility.

- Deuteronomy 30:19 (KJV): "I call heaven and earth to record this day against you, that I have set before you life and death, blessing and cursing: therefore choose life, that both thou and thy seed may live."

Biblical Foundations

The Bible consistently affirms the existence of free will, portraying humans as moral agents capable of making significant choices.

- Joshua 24:15 (KJV): "And if it seem evil unto you to serve the LORD, choose you this day whom ye will serve; whether the gods which your fathers served that were on the other side of the flood, or the gods of the Amorites, in whose land ye dwell: but as for me and my house, we will serve the LORD."

The Origin of Disobedience

The Fall of Adam and Eve

The story of Adam and Eve in the Garden of Eden is the archetypal narrative of free will leading to disobedience. Given the freedom to obey or disobey God's command, they chose the latter.

- Genesis 3:6 (KJV): "And when the woman saw that the tree was good for food, and that it was pleasant to the eyes, and a tree to be desired to make one wise, she took of the fruit thereof, and did eat, and gave also unto her husband with her; and he did eat."

The Role of Temptation

Temptation plays a crucial role in the exercise of free will and the choice to disobey. The serpent's deception in

Eden illustrates how external influences can lead to disobedience.

- Genesis 3:1-5 (KJV): "Now the serpent was more subtil than any beast of the field which the LORD God had made. And he said unto the woman, Yea, hath God said, Ye shall not eat of every tree of the garden? And the woman said unto the serpent, We may eat of the fruit of the trees of the garden: But of the fruit of the tree which is in the midst of the garden, God hath said, Ye shall not eat of it, neither shall ye touch it, lest ye die. And the serpent said unto the woman, Ye shall not surely die: For God doth know that in the day ye eat thereof, then your eyes shall be opened, and ye shall be as gods, knowing good and evil."

Biblical Examples of Disobedience

Cain and Abel

Cain's choice to kill his brother Abel is another early example of free will leading to disobedience. Despite God's warning, Cain chose to act on his anger and jealousy.

- Genesis 4:6-8 (KJV): "And the LORD said unto Cain, Why art thou wroth? and why is thy countenance fallen? If thou doest well, shalt thou not be accepted? and if thou doest not well, sin lieth at the door. And unto thee shall be his desire, and thou shalt rule over him. And Cain talked with Abel his brother: and it came to pass, when they were in the field, that Cain rose up against Abel his brother, and slew him."

The Israelites in the Wilderness

The Israelites' repeated disobedience during their journey through the wilderness, despite God's clear instructions and miraculous interventions, underscores the persistent challenge of free will and disobedience.

- Numbers 14:22-23 (KJV): "Because all those men which have seen my glory, and my miracles, which I did in Egypt and in the wilderness, and have tempted me now these ten times, and have not hearkened to my voice; Surely they shall not see the land which I sware unto their fathers, neither shall any of them that provoked me see it."

King Saul

King Saul's disobedience to God's commands, including sparing King Agag and the best of the livestock, illustrates the consequences of choosing personal judgment over divine instruction.

- 1 Samuel 15:22-23 (KJV): "And Samuel said, Hath the LORD as great delight in burnt offerings and sacrifices, as in obeying the voice of the LORD? Behold, to obey is better than sacrifice, and to hearken than the fat of rams. For rebellion is as the sin of witchcraft, and stubbornness is as iniquity and idolatry. Because thou hast rejected the word of the LORD, he hath also rejected thee from being king."

The Theological Implications of Disobedience

Sin and Separation from God

Disobedience is fundamentally an act of sin that results in separation from God. It reflects a refusal to trust and submit to God's authority.

- Isaiah 59:2 (KJV): "But your iniquities have separated between you and your God, and your sins have hid his face from you, that he will not hear."

Human Responsibility

The existence of free will means that individuals are responsible for their choices and the consequences of those choices. Disobedience, therefore, is not just a matter of human weakness but a deliberate choice.

- Romans 1:20 (KJV): "For the invisible things of him from the creation of the world are clearly seen, being understood by the things that are made, even his eternal power and Godhead; so that they are without excuse."

The Need for Redemption

The prevalence of disobedience underscores the need for redemption through Jesus Christ. Only through His sacrificial death and resurrection can the breach caused by disobedience be healed.

- Romans 5:18-19 (KJV): "Therefore as by the offence of one judgment came upon all men to condemnation; even so by the righteousness of one the free gift came upon all men unto justification of life. For as by one man's disobedience many were made sinners, so by the obedience of one shall many be made righteous."

Practical Reflections on Free Will and Disobedience

Recognizing Temptation

Understanding the role of free will in disobedience helps believers recognize and resist temptation. Being aware of the sources of temptation and the consequences of yielding to it is crucial.

- James 1:14-15 (KJV): "But every man is tempted, when he is drawn away of his own lust, and enticed. Then when lust hath conceived, it bringeth forth sin: and sin, when it is finished, bringeth forth death."

Seeking God's Guidance

Exercising free will responsibly requires seeking God's guidance through prayer, Scripture, and the counsel of wise believers. Aligning one's will with God's will is essential for avoiding disobedience.

- Psalm 119:105 (KJV): "Thy word is a lamp unto my feet, and a light unto my path."

Repentance and Forgiveness

When disobedience occurs, repentance and seeking God's forgiveness are critical. God's grace is sufficient to restore those who turn back to Him.

- 1 John 1:9 (KJV): "If we confess our sins, he is faithful and just to forgive us our sins, and to cleanse us from all unrighteousness."

Living in Obedience

Believers are called to live in obedience to God's commands, recognizing that true freedom is found in submission to God's will.

- John 14:15 (KJV): "If ye love me, keep my commandments."

Expository Study with Strong's Concordance

Obey ("שָׁמַע" shama)

The Hebrew word "שָׁמַע" (shama), Strong's H8085, means to hear, listen, or obey. It emphasizes attentive listening and responsive action.

- Deuteronomy 6:4 (KJV): "Hear, O Israel: The LORD our God is one LORD."

Disobey ("ἀπειθέω" apeitheo)

The Greek word "ἀπειθέω" (apeitheo), Strong's G544, means to disobey, be disobedient, or refuse to comply. It denotes a willful rejection of authority.

- John 3:36 (KJV): "He that believeth on the Son hath everlasting life: and he that believeth not the Son shall not see life; but the wrath of God abideth on him."

Comprehensive Commentary

Interpreting Free Will and Disobedience

The relationship between free will and disobedience highlights the complex nature of human moral agency. Free will is a gift that allows for genuine relationship and moral growth, but it also carries the risk of disobedience.

Balancing Freedom and Responsibility

Free will and disobedience must be understood within the context of divine grace and human responsibility. Believers are called to exercise their freedom responsibly, recognizing the consequences of their choices.

The Role of Community

Community plays a vital role in helping individuals navigate the challenges of free will and disobedience. Mutual accountability and support are essential for fostering obedience and resisting temptation.

- Hebrews 10:24-25 (KJV): "And let us consider one another to provoke unto love and to good works: Not forsaking the assembling of ourselves together, as the manner of some is; but exhorting one another: and so much the more, as ye see the day approaching."

The relationship between free will and disobedience is a central theme in the biblical narrative and Christian theology. Free will allows for genuine moral choices, but it also opens the possibility for disobedience. Understanding this relationship helps believers recognize the importance of seeking God's guidance, resisting temptation, and living in obedience to His will. This chapter has explored the interplay between free will and disobedience, providing a comprehensive understanding of their theological and practical implications.

Will There Be Free Will After Death?

The question of whether free will persists after death is a profound theological inquiry that touches on eschatology, the nature of the afterlife, and the eternal state of human beings. This chapter explores biblical perspectives and theological insights on the existence and nature of free will after death, examining how it relates to heaven, hell, and the ultimate fulfillment of God's redemptive plan.

The Nature of Free Will in the Afterlife

Biblical Foundations

The Bible provides glimpses into the nature of the afterlife, describing the eternal states of both the righteous and the wicked. However, it does not explicitly address the question of free will in these contexts.

- Revelation 21:3-4 (KJV): "And I heard a great voice out of heaven saying, Behold, the tabernacle of God is with men, and he will dwell with them, and they shall be his people, and God himself shall be with them, and be their God. And God shall wipe away all tears from their eyes; and there shall be no more death, neither sorrow, nor crying, neither shall there be any more pain: for the former things are passed away."

The Eternal States

Scripture describes two eternal destinies: heaven (or the new creation) and hell (or the lake of fire). The nature of existence in these states offers insights into the concept of free will.

- Matthew 25:46 (KJV): "And these shall go away into everlasting punishment: but the righteous into life eternal."

Free Will in Heaven

Perfection and Sinlessness

In heaven, or the new creation, believers will be made perfect and sinless. This perfection suggests a transformation of free will, where the inclination to sin is entirely removed.

- 1 John 3:2 (KJV): "Beloved, now are we the sons of God, and it doth not yet appear what we shall be: but we know that, when he shall appear, we shall be like him; for we shall see him as he is."

Willing Obedience and Joyful Service

The exercise of free will in heaven will align perfectly with God's will. Believers will joyfully and willingly serve God without the conflict of sinful desires.

- Revelation 22:3-4 (KJV): "And there shall be no more curse: but the throne of God and of the Lamb shall be in it; and his servants shall serve him: And they shall see his face; and his name shall be in their foreheads."

Eternal Fellowship with God

In heaven, free will is expressed through perfect fellowship with God, where love and worship flow freely and joyfully from the redeemed.

- Psalm 16:11 (KJV): "Thou wilt shew me the path of life: in thy presence is fulness of joy; at thy right hand there are pleasures for evermore."

Free Will in Hell

Eternal Separation and Consequences

Hell, described as a place of eternal separation from God, is the result of a final, irrevocable choice against God. The nature of existence in hell involves enduring the consequences of this choice.

- 2 Thessalonians 1:9 (KJV): "Who shall be punished with everlasting destruction from the presence of the Lord, and from the glory of his power."

The Fixity of the Eternal State

The biblical portrayal of hell suggests a fixed state where the opportunity for repentance and change no longer exists. Free will, in this context, has culminated in the finality of judgment.

- Luke 16:26 (KJV): "And beside all this, between us and you there is a great gulf fixed: so that they which would pass from hence to you cannot; neither can they pass to us, that would come from thence."

Continued Rebellion

Some theological perspectives suggest that the inhabitants of hell continue in their rebellion against God, reinforcing their separation and the consequences of their choices.

- Revelation 16:11 (KJV): "And blasphemed the God of heaven because of their pains and their sores, and repented not of their deeds."

Theological Implications of Free Will After Death

The Fulfillment of Redemption

For the redeemed, free will after death is perfected and fully aligned with God's will. This transformation is the fulfillment of God's redemptive work, where believers freely and joyfully choose to worship and serve Him forever.

- Romans 8:29-30 (KJV): "For whom he did foreknow, he also did predestinate to be conformed to the image of his Son, that he might be the firstborn among many brethren. Moreover whom he did predestinate, them he also called: and whom he called, them he also justified: and whom he justified, them he also glorified."

The Finality of Judgment

The finality of judgment in hell underscores the gravity of free will and the eternal consequences of rejecting God. It highlights the seriousness of moral choices and the enduring nature of divine justice.

- Hebrews 9:27 (KJV): "And as it is appointed unto men once to die, but after this the judgment."

God's Sovereignty and Human Choice

The existence of free will after death, particularly in heaven, reflects the harmony between God's sovereignty and human choice. Believers' perfected free will is a testament to God's ultimate purpose and plan for His creation.

- Ephesians 1:11 (KJV): "In whom also we have obtained an inheritance, being predestinated according to the purpose of him who worketh all things after the counsel of his own will."

Practical Reflections on Free Will After Death

Living with Eternity in Mind

Understanding the nature of free will after death encourages believers to live with an eternal perspective, making choices that reflect their ultimate destiny.

- Colossians 3:1-2 (KJV): "If ye then be risen with Christ, seek those things which are above, where Christ sitteth on the right hand of God. Set your affection on things above, not on things on the earth."

The Urgency of the Gospel

The finality of free will after death underscores the urgency of the gospel message. Believers are called to share the good news of salvation, knowing that eternal destinies are at stake.

- 2 Corinthians 5:20 (KJV): "Now then we are ambassadors for Christ, as though God did beseech you by us: we pray you in Christ's stead, be ye reconciled to God."

Comfort and Assurance for Believers

For believers, the promise of perfected free will in heaven provides comfort and assurance. It affirms that their struggles with sin and disobedience will one day be fully overcome.

- Philippians 1:6 (KJV): "Being confident of this very thing, that he which hath begun a good work in you will perform it until the day of Jesus Christ."

Expository Study with Strong's Concordance

Free Will ("ἐλεύθερος" eleutheros)

The Greek word "ἐλεύθερος" (eleutheros), Strong's G1658, means free or unrestrained. It denotes the state of being free from bondage or constraint, applicable to the redeemed state in heaven.

- Galatians 5:1 (KJV): "Stand fast therefore in the liberty wherewith Christ hath made us free, and be not entangled again with the yoke of bondage."

Eternal Life ("ζωὴ αἰώνιος" zoe aionios)

The Greek phrase "ζωὴ αἰώνιος" (zoe aionios), Strong's G166, means eternal life. It refers to the everlasting life promised to believers, characterized by perfect fellowship with God.

- John 3:16 (KJV): "For God so loved the world, that he gave his only begotten Son, that whosoever believeth in him should not perish, but have everlasting life."

Comprehensive Commentary

Interpreting Free Will in the Afterlife

The concept of free will in the afterlife is complex and multifaceted. In heaven, free will is perfected and fully aligned with God's will, while in hell, it culminates in the fixed state of separation and judgment.

The Role of Redemption and Judgment

Redemption transforms free will, enabling believers to eternally choose God without the conflict of sin. Judgment solidifies the consequences of rejecting God, emphasizing the eternal significance of free will.

The Harmony of Divine Sovereignty and Human Choice

The existence of free will after death reflects the harmony between divine sovereignty and human choice. It showcases God's ultimate purpose for His creation, where free will is exercised in perfect alignment with His will.

The question of whether free will persists after death is answered through a theological exploration of the eternal states of heaven and hell. In heaven, free will is perfected and aligned with God's will, leading to eternal joy and fellowship with Him. In hell, free will culminates in the fixed state of separation and enduring consequences of rejecting God. Understanding these realities encourages believers to live with an eternal perspective, share the gospel with urgency, and find comfort in the promise of redemption. This chapter has provided a comprehensive exploration of the nature of free will after death, its theological implications, and practical reflections for the Christian life.

This chapter has examined the concept of free will after death, laying the groundwork for further discussions on the implications of eternal destinies, the nature of divine justice and mercy, and the ultimate fulfillment of God's redemptive plan.

The next chapters will build on these insights, delving deeper into the theological and practical implications of the afterlife and the Christian hope.

CHAPTER 06

THE NATURE OF EVIL

Different Types of Evil: Moral, Natural, and Metaphysical

Evil is a pervasive reality that affects every aspect of human existence and the natural world. Understanding the nature of evil and its various forms is crucial for grappling with the problem of suffering, the human condition, and the need for redemption. This chapter explores the different types of evil—moral, natural, and metaphysical—providing a comprehensive understanding of their characteristics, origins, and theological implications.

Moral Evil

Definition of Moral Evil

Moral evil refers to the wrong actions and behaviors committed by free agents, typically humans, that result in harm, suffering, and injustice. It is rooted in the misuse of free will.

- Genesis 6:5 (KJV): "And God saw that the wickedness of man was great in the earth, and that every imagination of the thoughts of his heart was only evil continually."

Examples of Moral Evil

Moral evil encompasses a wide range of actions, including violence, theft, deceit, and oppression. Biblical narratives provide numerous examples of moral evil:

- Cain and Abel: Cain's murder of his brother Abel is a prime example of moral evil arising from jealousy and anger.

- Genesis 4:8 (KJV): "And Cain talked with Abel his brother: and it came to pass, when they were in the field, that Cain rose up against Abel his brother, and slew him."

- David and Bathsheba: King David's adultery with Bathsheba and the subsequent murder of her husband Uriah illustrate the devastating effects of moral evil.

- 2 Samuel 11:14-15 (KJV): "And it came to pass in the morning, that David wrote a letter to Joab, and sent it by the hand of Uriah. And he wrote in the letter, saying, Set ye

Uriah in the forefront of the hottest battle, and retire ye from him, that he may be smitten, and die."

Theological Implications of Moral Evil

Moral evil underscores the fallen nature of humanity and the misuse of free will. It reveals the need for moral accountability, repentance, and divine intervention to restore justice and righteousness.

- Romans 3:23 (KJV): "For all have sinned, and come short of the glory of God."

Natural Evil

Definition of Natural Evil

Natural evil refers to the suffering and harm resulting from natural processes and phenomena, such as natural disasters, diseases, and genetic disorders. Unlike moral evil, natural evil is not directly caused by human actions.

- Romans 8:22 (KJV): "For we know that the whole creation groaneth and travaileth in pain together until now."

Examples of Natural Evil

Natural evil includes a wide array of events and conditions that cause suffering:

- Natural Disasters: Earthquakes, hurricanes, floods, and tsunamis are examples of natural disasters that can cause immense suffering and loss of life.

- Diseases and Illnesses: Cancer, genetic disorders, and pandemics are examples of natural evil that impact human health and well-being.

Theological Implications of Natural Evil

Natural evil raises profound questions about the nature of creation and God's sovereignty. It highlights the brokenness of the world and the need for restoration. The presence of natural evil is often understood in light of the fall and the resulting curse on creation.

- Genesis 3:17-18 (KJV): "And unto Adam he said, Because thou hast hearkened unto the voice of thy wife, and hast eaten of the tree, of which I commanded thee, saying, Thou shalt not eat of it: cursed is the ground for thy sake; in sorrow shalt thou eat of it all the days of thy life; Thorns also and thistles shall it bring forth to thee; and thou shalt eat the herb of the field."

Metaphysical Evil

Definition of Metaphysical Evil

Metaphysical evil refers to the inherent limitations and imperfections within creation. It includes the finitude, fragility, and dependency of all created beings, which can lead to suffering and imperfection.

Examples of Metaphysical Evil

Metaphysical evil encompasses the fundamental constraints of existence:

- Finitude and Mortality: The fact that all living beings are finite and subject to death is a form of metaphysical evil.

- Imperfection: The inherent imperfections and limitations in all aspects of creation, including the human mind and body, reflect metaphysical evil.

Theological Implications of Metaphysical Evil

Metaphysical evil raises questions about the nature of existence and the purpose of creation. It highlights the distinction between the Creator and the created, emphasizing the need for divine grace and the hope of ultimate perfection in God's eternal plan.

- 1 Corinthians 15:42-44 (KJV): "So also is the resurrection of the dead. It is sown in corruption; it is raised in incorruption: It is sown in dishonour; it is raised in glory: it is sown in weakness; it is raised in power: It is sown a natural body; it is raised a spiritual body. There is a natural body, and there is a spiritual body."

The Interplay of Different Types of Evil

Interaction Between Moral and Natural Evil

Moral and natural evil often intersect, with human actions exacerbating natural disasters and their consequences. For example, deforestation can increase the severity of floods, and poor infrastructure can magnify the impact of earthquakes.

Metaphysical Evil and the Human Condition

Metaphysical evil underpins both moral and natural evil, providing the framework within which they occur. The limitations and imperfections inherent in creation set the stage for both moral failures and natural catastrophes.

The Hope of Redemption

Despite the pervasive presence of evil, the Christian hope lies in the promise of redemption and the ultimate defeat of all forms of evil. Through Jesus Christ, God offers a path to overcome moral evil, heal natural evil, and transcend metaphysical evil.

- Revelation 21:4 (KJV): "And God shall wipe away all tears from their eyes; and there shall be no more death, neither sorrow, nor crying, neither shall there be any more pain: for the former things are passed away."

Practical Reflections on the Nature of Evil

Responding to Moral Evil

Believers are called to confront moral evil through righteous living, advocacy for justice, and acts of compassion. Personal and communal repentance are essential in addressing moral failings.

- Micah 6:8 (KJV): "He hath shewed thee, O man, what is good; and what doth the LORD require of thee, but to do justly, and to love mercy, and to walk humbly with thy God?"

Dealing with Natural Evil

Responding to natural evil involves practical measures such as disaster preparedness, medical care, and environmental stewardship. It also requires spiritual resilience and trust in God's sovereignty.

- Psalm 46:1-2 (KJV): "God is our refuge and strength, a very present help in trouble. Therefore will not we fear, though the earth be removed, and though the mountains be carried into the midst of the sea."

Embracing the Hope of Redemption

In the face of metaphysical evil, believers are called to embrace the hope of resurrection and the promise of a new creation. This hope encourages perseverance and faithfulness in the present life.

- Romans 8:18 (KJV): "For I reckon that the sufferings of this present time are not worthy to be compared with the glory which shall be revealed in us."

Expository Study with Strong's Concordance

Evil ("רָע" ra)

The Hebrew word "רָע" (ra), Strong's H7451, means evil, wickedness, or calamity. It encompasses both moral and natural evil.

- Genesis 6:5 (KJV): "And God saw that the wickedness of man was great in the earth, and that every imagination of the thoughts of his heart was only evil continually."

Suffering ("πάσχω" pascho)

The Greek word "πάσχω" (pascho), Strong's G3958, means to suffer or undergo hardship. It reflects the experience of natural and metaphysical evil.

- 1 Peter 4:19 (KJV): "Wherefore let them that suffer according to the will of God commit the keeping of their souls to him in well doing, as unto a faithful Creator."

Comprehensive Commentary

Interpreting the Nature of Evil

Understanding the different types of evil—moral, natural, and metaphysical—provides a comprehensive framework for grappling with the problem of evil. Each type has distinct characteristics and theological implications, yet they are interconnected in the fallen state of creation.

The Role of Free Will and the Fall

Free will plays a critical role in the manifestation of moral evil, while the fall of humanity explains the introduction of both natural and metaphysical evil into the world. These realities underscore the need for redemption and the hope of restoration.

The Hope of Restoration and Redemption

Christian theology offers the promise of restoration through Jesus Christ, who will ultimately defeat all forms of evil. This hope provides a foundation for resilience, faith, and active engagement in addressing the effects of evil in the present world.

The nature of evil is multifaceted, encompassing moral, natural, and metaphysical dimensions. Each type of evil has distinct characteristics and theological implications, yet they are interconnected within the fallen state of creation. Understanding these different types of evil is crucial for grappling with the problem of suffering, the human condition, and the need for redemption.

This chapter has provided a comprehensive exploration of the nature of evil, laying the groundwork for further discussions on the implications of evil and the hope of redemption through Jesus Christ.

The Role of Satan and Demonic Forces in Christian Theology

Satan and demonic forces play a significant role in Christian theology, representing the embodiment of evil and opposition to God's purposes. This chapter explores the nature, origin, and activities of Satan and demons, their influence on the world, and the theological implications of their existence. Understanding the role of these forces is crucial for grasping the full scope of spiritual warfare, the human condition, and the redemptive work of Jesus Christ.

The Nature and Origin of Satan

The Creation and Fall of Satan

Satan, originally created as a powerful and beautiful angel, fell from his exalted position due to pride and rebellion against God. The Bible provides glimpses into his origin and fall.

- Isaiah 14:12-15 (KJV): "How art thou fallen from heaven, O Lucifer, son of the morning! how art thou cut down to the ground, which didst weaken the nations! For thou hast said in thine heart, I will ascend into heaven, I will exalt my throne above the stars of God: I will sit also upon the mount of the congregation, in the sides of the north: I will ascend above the heights of the clouds; I will be like the most High. Yet thou shalt be brought down to hell, to the sides of the pit."

- Ezekiel 28:12-17 (KJV): "Son of man, take up a lamentation upon the king of Tyrus, and say unto him, Thus saith the Lord GOD; Thou sealest up the sum, full of wisdom, and perfect in beauty. Thou hast been in Eden the garden of God; every precious stone was thy covering...Thou wast perfect in thy ways from the day that thou wast created, till iniquity was found in thee. By the multitude of thy merchandise they have filled the midst of thee with violence, and thou hast sinned: therefore I will cast thee as profane out of the mountain of God: and I will destroy thee, O covering cherub, from the midst of the stones of fire."

Names and Titles of Satan

The Bible uses various names and titles to describe Satan, each reflecting different aspects of his character and activities.

- Adversary (Satan): Emphasizing his role as the opponent of God and humanity.

- 1 Peter 5:8 (KJV): "Be sober, be vigilant; because your adversary the devil, as a roaring lion, walketh about, seeking whom he may devour."

- Devil (Diabolos): Meaning "slanderer" or "accuser."

- Revelation 12:10 (KJV): "And I heard a loud voice saying in heaven, Now is come salvation, and strength, and the kingdom of our God, and the power of his Christ: for the accuser of our brethren is cast down, which accused them before our God day and night."

- Serpent: Reflecting his deceitful and cunning nature.

- Genesis 3:1 (KJV): "Now the serpent was more subtil than any beast of the field which the LORD God had made. And he said unto the woman, Yea, hath God said, Ye shall not eat of every tree of the garden?"

- Prince of the Power of the Air: Indicating his influence over the world.

- Ephesians 2:2 (KJV): "Wherein in time past ye walked according to the course of this world, according to the prince of the power of the air, the spirit that now worketh in the children of disobedience."

The Nature and Activities of Demonic Forces

Creation and Fall of Demons

Demonic forces, also known as fallen angels, followed Satan in his rebellion against God. They were originally created as good angels but chose to rebel and were cast out of heaven.

- Revelation 12:4 (KJV): "And his tail drew the third part of the stars of heaven, and did cast them to the earth."

Characteristics and Abilities

Demons possess various characteristics and abilities, including intelligence, strength, and the ability to influence and possess humans.

- Matthew 8:28-32 (KJV): "And when he was come to the other side into the country of the Gergesenes, there met him two possessed with devils, coming out of the tombs, exceeding fierce, so that no man might pass by that way. And, behold, they cried out, saying, What have we to do with thee, Jesus, thou Son of God? art thou come hither to torment us before the time?...And he said unto them, Go. And when they were come out, they went into the herd of swine: and, behold, the whole herd of swine ran violently down a steep place into the sea, and perished in the waters."

Activities and Influence

Demons engage in various activities to oppose God's purposes and harm humanity. These include temptation, deception, possession, and inciting rebellion against God.

- Ephesians 6:12 (KJV): "For we wrestle not against flesh and blood, but against principalities, against powers, against the rulers of the darkness of this world, against spiritual wickedness in high places."

The Influence of Satan and Demonic Forces on the World

Temptation and Deception

Satan and his demons actively seek to tempt and deceive humans, leading them away from God's truth and into sin.

- Genesis 3:1-5 (KJV): "Now the serpent was more subtil than any beast of the field which the LORD God had made. And he said unto the woman, Yea, hath God said, Ye shall not eat of every tree of the garden? And the woman said unto the serpent, We may eat of the fruit of the trees of the garden: But of the fruit of the tree which is in the midst of the garden, God hath said, Ye shall not eat of it, neither shall ye touch it, lest ye die. And the serpent said unto the woman, Ye shall not surely die: For God doth know that in the day ye eat thereof, then your eyes shall be opened, and ye shall be as gods, knowing good and evil."

- John 8:44 (KJV): "Ye are of your father the devil, and the lusts of your father ye will do. He was a murderer from the beginning, and abode not in the truth, because there is no truth in him. When he speaketh a lie, he speaketh of his own: for he is a liar, and the father of it."

Possession and Oppression

Demonic possession and oppression are ways in which demons exert direct influence over individuals, causing physical, mental, and spiritual harm.

- Mark 5:2-5 (KJV): "And when he was come out of the ship, immediately there met him out of the tombs a man with an unclean spirit, Who had his dwelling among the tombs; and no man could bind him, no, not with chains: Because that he had been often bound with fetters and chains, and the chains had been plucked asunder by him, and the fetters broken in pieces: neither could any man tame him. And always, night and day, he was in the mountains, and in the tombs, crying, and cutting himself with stones."

Sowing Division and Conflict

Satan and demons seek to sow division, conflict, and chaos in the world, undermining unity and peace.

- James 3:14-16 (KJV): "But if ye have bitter envying and strife in your hearts, glory not, and lie not against the truth. This wisdom descendeth not from above, but is earthly, sensual, devilish. For where envying and strife is, there is confusion and every evil work."

Theological Implications of Satan and Demonic Forces

The Reality of Spiritual Warfare

The existence of Satan and demonic forces underscores the reality of spiritual warfare. Believers are called to be vigilant, discerning, and equipped with spiritual armor to stand against these forces.

- Ephesians 6:10-11 (KJV): "Finally, my brethren, be strong in the Lord, and in the power of his might. Put on the whole armour of God, that ye may be able to stand against the wiles of the devil."

The Need for Redemption and Deliverance

The pervasive influence of Satan and demons highlights the need for redemption and deliverance through Jesus Christ. His victory over these forces provides believers with the power to resist and overcome.

- Colossians 2:15 (KJV): "And having spoiled principalities and powers, he made a shew of them openly, triumphing over them in it."

The Sovereignty of God

Despite the active opposition of Satan and demons, God's sovereignty remains supreme. He uses even the actions of these forces to accomplish His ultimate purposes and demonstrate His glory.

- Romans 8:28 (KJV): "And we know that all things work together for good to them that love God, to them who are the called according to his purpose."

Practical Reflections on Spiritual Warfare

Vigilance and Discernment

Believers must be vigilant and discerning, recognizing the tactics of Satan and demons and standing firm in their faith.

- 1 Peter 5:8-9 (KJV): "Be sober, be vigilant; because your adversary the devil, as a roaring lion, walketh about, seeking whom he may devour: Whom resist stedfast in the faith, knowing that the same afflictions are accomplished in your brethren that are in the world."

Prayer and Spiritual Armor

Engaging in spiritual warfare requires the use of prayer and the spiritual armor provided by God. This includes truth, righteousness, faith, salvation, the Word of God, and prayer.

- Ephesians 6:13-18 (KJV): "Wherefore take unto you the whole armour of God, that ye may be able to withstand in the evil day, and having done all, to stand. Stand therefore, having your loins girt about with truth, and having on the breastplate of righteousness; And your feet shod with the preparation of the gospel of peace; Above all, taking the shield of faith, wherewith ye shall be able to quench all the fiery darts of the wicked. And take the helmet of salvation, and the sword of the Spirit, which is the word of God: Praying always with all prayer and supplication in the Spirit, and watching thereunto with all perseverance and supplication for all saints."

Resisting Temptation and Deception

Believers must actively resist temptation and deception, relying on God's strength and wisdom to stand firm against the lies and schemes of the enemy.

- James 4:7 (KJV): "Submit yourselves therefore to God. Resist the devil, and he will flee from you."

Expository Study with Strong's Concordance

Devil ("διάβολος" diabolos)

The Greek word "διάβολος" (diabolos), Strong's G1228, means slanderer or accuser. It is used to describe Satan's role in opposing and accusing believers.

- 1 Peter 5:8 (KJV): "Be sober, be vigilant; because your adversary the devil, as a roaring lion, walketh about, seeking whom he may devour."

Demon ("δαιμόνιον" daimonion)

The Greek word "δαιμόνιον" (daimonion), Strong's G1140, means demon or evil spirit. It refers to the fallen angels who serve Satan and oppose God's purposes.

- Mark 5:12 (KJV): "And all the devils besought him, saying, Send us into the swine, that we may enter into them."

Comprehensive Commentary

Interpreting the Role of Satan and Demonic Forces

Understanding the role of Satan and demonic forces is essential for grasping the full scope of spiritual warfare and the human condition. These forces actively oppose God's purposes and seek to harm humanity, yet they operate under the sovereign control of God.

Balancing Awareness and Confidence

Believers are called to be aware of the reality of Satan and demonic forces without succumbing to fear. Confidence in Christ's victory and the power of the Holy Spirit provides the foundation for resisting and overcoming these forces.

The Ultimate Defeat of Evil

The ultimate defeat of Satan and demonic forces is assured through the redemptive work of Jesus Christ. This victory will be fully realized in the eschaton, when all evil is vanquished, and God's kingdom is established in its fullness.

- Revelation 20:10 (KJV): "And the devil that deceived them was cast into the lake of fire and brimstone, where the beast and the false prophet are, and shall be tormented day and night for ever and ever."

The role of Satan and demonic forces in Christian theology is crucial for understanding the reality of evil, spiritual warfare, and the need for redemption. These forces actively oppose God's purposes and seek to deceive, tempt, and harm humanity. However, through Jesus Christ, believers have the power to resist and overcome these forces. This chapter has provided a comprehensive exploration of the nature, origin, activities, and influence of Satan and demonic forces, offering theological insights and practical reflections for the Christian life.

If There's No Sin in Heaven, How Did Lucifer Disobey and Go Against God?

The rebellion of Lucifer, who became Satan, raises profound theological questions, especially considering the belief that there is no sin in heaven. This chapter explores the origins of Lucifer's disobedience, the nature of sin and free will, and how this event fits within the broader framework of Christian theology. Understanding Lucifer's fall provides insight into the complexities of free will, the presence of evil, and God's sovereignty.

The Nature of Lucifer's Rebellion

Lucifer's Original State

Lucifer, often identified with the "morning star" or "light-bringer," was created as a powerful and beautiful angel. He held a high position among the heavenly hosts.

- Ezekiel 28:12-15 (KJV): "Son of man, take up a lamentation upon the king of Tyrus, and say unto him, Thus saith the Lord GOD; Thou sealest up the sum, full of wisdom, and perfect in beauty. Thou hast been in Eden the garden of God; every precious stone was thy covering...Thou art the anointed cherub that covereth; and I have set thee so: thou wast upon the holy mountain of God; thou hast walked up and down in the midst of the stones of fire. Thou wast perfect in thy ways from the day that thou wast created, till iniquity was found in thee."

The Nature of Free Will in Angels

Like humans, angels were created with free will. This ability to choose is essential for genuine love and obedience to God. However, it also allows for the possibility of rebellion.

The Rebellion of Lucifer

Lucifer's rebellion stemmed from pride and a desire to exalt himself above God. This desire led to his fall from grace.

- Isaiah 14:12-14 (KJV): "How art thou fallen from heaven, O Lucifer, son of the morning! how art thou cut down to the ground, which didst weaken the nations! For thou hast said in thine heart, I will ascend into heaven, I will exalt my throne above the stars of God: I will sit also upon the mount of the congregation, in the sides of the north: I will ascend above the heights of the clouds; I will be like the most High."

The Presence of Sin and Free Will in Heaven

Understanding Sin in Heaven

While heaven is characterized by the absence of sin among its inhabitants, the initial presence of free will allowed for the possibility of rebellion. Sin entered through the free choice of Lucifer and the angels who followed him.

The Role of Free Will

Free will is integral to the nature of created beings, both human and angelic. It enables genuine love and worship but also allows for the possibility of disobedience.

- Jude 1:6 (KJV): "And the angels which kept not their first estate, but left their own habitation, he hath reserved in everlasting chains under darkness unto the judgment of the great day."

The Sovereignty of God

God's sovereignty includes the allowance of free will. Lucifer's rebellion did not thwart God's ultimate plan but rather highlighted the need for divine justice and the unfolding of His redemptive purposes.

Theological Implications of Lucifer's Fall

The Nature of Pride and Rebellion

Lucifer's fall illustrates the destructive nature of pride and the dangers of self-exaltation. It serves as a warning against similar attitudes in humanity.

- Proverbs 16:18 (KJV): "Pride goeth before destruction, and an haughty spirit before a fall."

The Reality of Spiritual Warfare

The fall of Lucifer and the ongoing activity of Satan highlight the reality of spiritual warfare. Believers are called to be vigilant and equipped to resist these forces.

- Ephesians 6:12 (KJV): "For we wrestle not against flesh and blood, but against principalities, against powers, against the rulers of the darkness of this world, against spiritual wickedness in high places."

God's Justice and Redemption

Lucifer's rebellion set the stage for the demonstration of God's justice in punishing sin and His mercy in providing redemption for humanity.

- Colossians 2:15 (KJV): "And having spoiled principalities and powers, he made a shew of them openly, triumphing over them in it."

The Consequences of Lucifer's Rebellion

Expulsion from Heaven

Lucifer and the angels who rebelled with him were expelled from heaven, losing their positions and being cast down to earth.

- Revelation 12:7-9 (KJV): "And there was war in heaven: Michael and his angels fought against the dragon; and the dragon fought and his angels, And prevailed not; neither was their place found any more in heaven. And the great dragon was cast out, that old serpent, called the Devil, and Satan, which deceiveth the whole world: he was cast out into the earth, and his angels were cast out with him."

The Introduction of Evil into the World

Satan's influence led to the introduction of sin into the human realm, beginning with the temptation of Adam and Eve in the Garden of Eden.

- Genesis 3:1-5 (KJV): "Now the serpent was more subtil than any beast of the field which the LORD God had made. And he said unto the woman, Yea, hath God said, Ye shall not eat of every tree of the garden? And the woman said unto the serpent, We may eat of the fruit of the trees of the garden: But of the fruit of the tree which is in the midst of the garden, God hath said, Ye shall not eat of it, neither shall ye touch it, lest ye die. And the serpent said unto the woman, Ye shall not surely die: For God doth know that in the day ye eat thereof, then your eyes shall be opened, and ye shall be as gods, knowing good and evil."

Ongoing Spiritual Battle

Satan's rebellion initiated an ongoing spiritual battle between the forces of good and evil, influencing the lives and destinies of individuals and nations.

- 1 Peter 5:8 (KJV): "Be sober, be vigilant; because your adversary the devil, as a roaring lion, walketh about, seeking whom he may devour."

Practical Reflections on Lucifer's Fall

The Danger of Pride

Lucifer's fall serves as a stark reminder of the dangers of pride and self-exaltation. Believers are called to cultivate humility and dependence on God.

- James 4:6 (KJV): "But he giveth more grace. Wherefore he saith, God resisteth the proud, but giveth grace unto the humble."

Vigilance in Spiritual Warfare

Understanding the nature of Lucifer's rebellion underscores the importance of vigilance in spiritual warfare. Believers must be equipped with the armor of God to stand against the schemes of the enemy.

- Ephesians 6:13-18 (KJV): "Wherefore take unto you the whole armour of God, that ye may be able to withstand in the evil day, and having done all, to stand. Stand therefore, having your loins girt about with truth, and having on the breastplate of righteousness; And your feet shod with the preparation of the gospel of peace; Above all, taking the shield of faith, wherewith ye shall be able to quench all the fiery darts of the wicked. And take the helmet of salvation, and the sword of the Spirit, which is the word of God: Praying always with all prayer and supplication in the Spirit, and watching thereunto with all perseverance and supplication for all saints."

Hope in Redemption

Despite the reality of Satan's rebellion and the presence of evil, believers find hope in the redemptive work of Christ, who has triumphed over the forces of darkness and offers eternal life.

- Romans 16:20 (KJV): "And the God of peace shall bruise Satan under your feet shortly. The grace of our Lord Jesus Christ be with you. Amen."

Expository Study with Strong's Concordance

Pride ("גָּאוֹן" ga'own)

The Hebrew word "גָּאוֹן" (ga'own), Strong's H1344, means arrogance, pride, or majesty. It highlights the root cause of Lucifer's rebellion.

- Proverbs 16:18 (KJV): "Pride goeth before destruction, and an haughty spirit before a fall."

Rebellion ("מְרִי" meri)

The Hebrew word "מְרִי" (meri), Strong's H4805, means rebellion or disobedience. It describes the fundamental act of defiance against God's authority.

- 1 Samuel 15:23 (KJV): "For rebellion is as the sin of witchcraft, and stubbornness is as iniquity and idolatry. Because thou hast rejected the word of the LORD, he hath also rejected thee from being king."

Comprehensive Commentary

Interpreting Lucifer's Fall

Lucifer's fall is a profound theological event that illustrates the complexities of free will, the nature of sin, and the consequences of rebellion. It highlights the reality of spiritual warfare and the ongoing battle between good and evil.

The Balance of Free Will and Divine Sovereignty

The existence of free will among angels, including Lucifer, demonstrates God's desire for genuine love and obedience. Despite the rebellion, God's sovereignty ensures that His ultimate purposes will be fulfilled.

The Role of Redemption

The fall of Lucifer underscores the need for redemption and the hope found in Jesus Christ

His victory over sin and death provides the basis for overcoming the effects of rebellion and restoring the created order.

The question of how Lucifer could disobey and go against God, despite the absence of sin in heaven, is addressed by understanding the nature of free will and the potential for rebellion. Lucifer's fall highlights the dangers of pride and self-exaltation, the reality of spiritual warfare, and the need for vigilance and reliance on God's grace. This chapter has provided a comprehensive exploration of Lucifer's rebellion, its theological implications, and practical reflections for the Christian life.

The Nature of Sin and Free Will in Heaven

The rebellion of Lucifer and the subsequent fall of other angels raise important theological questions about the nature of free will and the existence of sin in heaven. This chapter explores whether sin existed in heaven before it was committed, the nature of angelic free will, and the implications of their ability to choose apart from God.

The Nature of Sin and Its Origin

Defining Sin

Sin is fundamentally an act of disobedience against God's will. It involves a deviation from the moral and divine law established by God.

- 1 John 3:4 (KJV): "Whosoever committeth sin transgresseth also the law: for sin is the transgression of the law."

The Concept of Sin in Heaven

Heaven is traditionally understood as a place of perfect holiness and communion with God. However, the possibility of sin arose through the exercise of free will by angels, including Lucifer.

- Ezekiel 28:15 (KJV): "Thou wast perfect in thy ways from the day that thou wast created, till iniquity was found in thee."

The Origin of Sin with Lucifer

Sin entered through the pride and rebellion of Lucifer, who chose to exalt himself above God. This choice marked the first act of sin in the heavenly realm.

- Isaiah 14:12-14 (KJV): "How art thou fallen from heaven, O Lucifer, son of the morning! how art thou cut down to the ground, which didst weaken the nations! For thou hast said in thine heart, I will ascend into heaven, I will exalt my throne above the stars of God: I will sit also upon the mount of the congregation, in the sides of the north: I will ascend above the heights of the clouds; I will be like the most High."

The Nature of Free Will in Angels

Free Will and Moral Agency

Free will is essential for genuine moral agency. It allows for the possibility of making meaningful choices, including the choice to obey or disobey God.

- Deuteronomy 30:19 (KJV): "I call heaven and earth to record this day against you, that I have set before you life and death, blessing and cursing: therefore choose life, that both thou and thy seed may live."

Angelic Free Will

Angels, like humans, were created with the ability to choose. This capacity for free will means that they can either remain in alignment with God's will or rebel against it.

- Jude 1:6 (KJV): "And the angels which kept not their first estate, but left their own habitation, he hath reserved in everlasting chains under darkness unto the judgment of the great day."

The Second Choice: Rebellion

The choice apart from God for angels is essentially rebellion. Lucifer's decision to rebel was rooted in pride and a desire for self-exaltation, leading to his fall.

- Ezekiel 28:17 (KJV): "Thine heart was lifted up because of thy beauty, thou hast corrupted thy wisdom by reason of thy brightness: I will cast thee to the ground, I will lay thee before kings, that they may behold thee."

Theological Implications of Angelic Free Will and Sin

The Potential for Sin

The presence of free will inherently includes the potential for sin. While heaven is a realm of holiness, the free will given to angels made the possibility of rebellion a reality.

The Distinction Between Potential and Actual Sin

Sin did not exist in heaven until it was committed by Lucifer. The potential for sin was inherent in the gift of free will, but it became actualized through Lucifer's choice.

God's Sovereignty and Free Will

God's sovereignty encompasses the allowance of free will. Lucifer's rebellion did not thwart God's ultimate plan but rather highlighted the necessity of divine justice and the unfolding of redemption.

- Romans 8:28 (KJV): "And we know that all things work together for good to them that love God, to them who are the called according to his purpose."

The Consequences of Angelic Rebellion

Expulsion from Heaven

Lucifer and the angels who followed him were expelled from heaven, losing their positions and being cast down to earth.

- Revelation 12:7-9 (KJV): "And there was war in heaven: Michael and his angels fought against the dragon; and the dragon fought and his angels, And prevailed not; neither was their place found any more in heaven. And the great dragon was cast out, that old serpent, called the Devil, and Satan, which deceiveth the whole world: he was cast out into the earth, and his angels were cast out with him."

Introduction of Evil

Satan's rebellion introduced evil into the created order, impacting not only the spiritual realm but also the physical world, as seen in the temptation and fall of humanity.

- Genesis 3:1-5 (KJV): "Now the serpent was more subtil than any beast of the field which the LORD God had made. And he said unto the woman, Yea, hath God said, Ye shall not eat of every tree of the garden? And the woman said unto the serpent, We may eat of the fruit of the trees of the garden: But of the fruit of the tree which is in the midst of the garden, God hath said, Ye shall not eat of it, neither shall ye touch it, lest ye die. And the serpent said unto the woman, Ye shall not surely die: For God doth know that in the day ye eat thereof, then your eyes shall be opened, and ye shall be as gods, knowing good and evil."

Ongoing Spiritual Conflict

The rebellion initiated an ongoing spiritual conflict between the forces of good and evil, influencing the lives and destinies of individuals and nations.

- Ephesians 6:12 (KJV): "For we wrestle not against flesh and blood, but against principalities, against powers, against the rulers of the darkness of this world, against spiritual wickedness in high places."

Practical Reflections on Angelic Free Will and Sin

Understanding the Nature of Free Will

Recognizing that free will includes the potential for both obedience and rebellion helps believers understand the importance of their choices and the need for alignment with God's will.

- Joshua 24:15 (KJV): "And if it seem evil unto you to serve the LORD, choose you this day whom ye will serve; whether the gods which your fathers served that were on the other side of the flood, or the gods of the Amorites, in whose land ye dwell: but as for me and my house, we will serve the LORD."

The Importance of Humility

Lucifer's fall underscores the dangers of pride and self-exaltation. Believers are called to cultivate humility and dependence on God.

- James 4:6 (KJV): "But he giveth more grace. Wherefore he saith, God resisteth the proud, but giveth grace unto the humble."

Engaging in Spiritual Warfare

Understanding the nature of angelic rebellion highlights the reality of spiritual warfare. Believers must be vigilant and equipped with the spiritual armor provided by God to stand against the forces of darkness.

- Ephesians 6:13-18 (KJV): "Wherefore take unto you the whole armour of God, that ye may be able to withstand in the evil day, and having done all, to stand. Stand therefore, having your loins girt about with truth, and having on the breastplate of righteousness; And your feet shod with the preparation of the gospel of peace; Above all, taking the shield of faith, wherewith ye shall be able to quench all the fiery darts of the wicked. And take the helmet of salvation, and the sword of the Spirit, which is the word of God: Praying always with all prayer and supplication in the Spirit, and watching thereunto with all perseverance and supplication for all saints."

Hope in Christ's Victory

Despite the rebellion and presence of evil, believers find hope in the victory of Jesus Christ, who has triumphed over sin and death and provides the basis for ultimate restoration.

- Colossians 2:15 (KJV): "And having spoiled principalities and powers, he made a shew of them openly, triumphing over them in it."

Expository Study with Strong's Concordance

Pride ("גָּאוֹן" ga'own)

The Hebrew word "גָּאוֹן" (ga'own), Strong's H1344, means arrogance, pride, or majesty. It highlights the root cause of Lucifer's rebellion.

- Proverbs 16:18 (KJV): "Pride goeth before destruction, and an haughty spirit before a fall."

Rebellion ("מְרִי" meri)

The Hebrew word "מְרִי" (meri), Strong's H4805, means rebellion or disobedience. It describes the fundamental act of defiance against God's authority.

- 1 Samuel 15:23 (KJV): "For rebellion is as the sin of witchcraft, and stubbornness is as iniquity and idolatry. Because thou hast rejected the word of the LORD, he hath also rejected thee from being king."

Comprehensive Commentary

Interpreting the Potential for Sin in Heaven

The potential for sin in heaven existed due to the gift of free will given to angels. Sin was actualized through Lucifer's choice to rebel, demonstrating the inherent risks of free moral agency.

Balancing Free Will and Divine Sovereignty

The existence of free will among angels, including Lucifer, illustrates the balance between God's sovereignty and the capacity for meaningful choice. Despite rebellion, God's ultimate plan remains intact and sovereign.

The Role of Redemption and Restoration

Lucifer's fall highlights the need for redemption and restoration through Jesus Christ. His victory over sin and death provides the foundation for overcoming rebellion and achieving ultimate reconciliation with God.

The question of whether sin existed in heaven before it was committed is addressed by understanding the nature of free will and the potential for rebellion. While heaven is a realm of holiness, the free will given to angels made the possibility of sin a reality, actualized through Lucifer's choice. This chapter has provided a comprehensive exploration of angelic free will, the origin of sin, and the theological implications of these concepts, offering practical reflections for the Christian life.

CHAPTER 07

HUMAN RESPONSIBILITY AND MORAL AGENCY

Human responsibility and moral agency are central themes in Christian theology, highlighting the significance of free will, accountability, and ethical decision-making. This chapter explores the concept of moral agency, its biblical foundations, and the implications of human accountability. Understanding moral agency is crucial for recognizing the role of humans as responsible agents in God's creation, capable of making choices that align with or deviate from divine will.

The Concept of Moral Agency

Definition of Moral Agency

Moral agency refers to the capacity of individuals to make moral judgments and be held accountable for their actions. It encompasses the ability to discern right from wrong and to act upon that knowledge.

- Genesis 2:16-17 (KJV): "And the LORD God commanded the man, saying, Of every tree of the garden thou mayest freely eat: But of the tree of the knowledge of good and evil, thou shalt not eat of it: for in the day that thou eatest thereof thou shalt surely die."

Biblical Foundations of Moral Agency

The Bible affirms human beings as moral agents created in the image of God, endowed with free will and the capacity for ethical decision-making.

- Genesis 1:26-27 (KJV): "And God said, Let us make man in our image, after our likeness: and let them have dominion over the fish of the sea, and over the fowl of the air, and over the cattle, and over all the earth, and over every creeping thing that creepeth upon the earth. So God created man in his own image, in the image of God created he him; male and female created he them."

The Role of Conscience

Conscience plays a critical role in moral agency, acting as an internal guide that helps individuals discern right from wrong and motivates them to act ethically.

- Romans 2:14-15 (KJV): "For when the Gentiles, which have not the law, do by nature the things contained in the law, these, having not the law, are a law unto themselves: Which shew the work of the law written in their hearts, their conscience also bearing witness, and their thoughts the mean while accusing or else excusing one another."

Human Accountability

Accountability to God

Humans are ultimately accountable to God for their actions. This accountability underscores the seriousness of moral choices and the consequences of sin.

- Ecclesiastes 12:14 (KJV): "For God shall bring every work into judgment, with every secret thing, whether it be good, or whether it be evil."

Accountability in Relationships

Humans are also accountable to one another within relationships and communities. This accountability promotes ethical behavior and social harmony.

- Galatians 6:1-2 (KJV): "Brethren, if a man be overtaken in a fault, ye which are spiritual, restore such an one in the spirit of meekness; considering thyself, lest thou also be tempted. Bear ye one another's burdens, and so fulfil the law of Christ."

The Consequences of Actions

The Bible teaches that actions have consequences, both temporal and eternal. Moral accountability involves facing the outcomes of one's choices.

- Galatians 6:7-8 (KJV): "Be not deceived; God is not mocked: for whatsoever a man soweth, that shall he also reap. For he that soweth to his flesh shall of the flesh reap corruption; but he that soweth to the Spirit shall of the Spirit reap life everlasting."

Theological Implications of Moral Agency

Free Will and Divine Sovereignty

Moral agency highlights the interplay between human free will and divine sovereignty. While God is sovereign, He grants humans the freedom to make moral choices, emphasizing personal responsibility.

- Deuteronomy 30:19-20 (KJV): "I call heaven and earth to record this day against you, that I have set before you life and death, blessing and cursing: therefore choose life, that both thou and thy seed may live: That thou mayest love the LORD thy God, and that thou mayest obey his voice, and that thou mayest cleave unto him: for he is thy life, and the length of thy days: that thou mayest dwell in the land which the LORD sware unto thy fathers, to Abraham, to Isaac, and to Jacob, to give them."

The Nature of Sin and Redemption

Understanding moral agency is essential for comprehending the nature of sin and the need for redemption. Human beings are responsible for their sinful actions and in need of salvation through Jesus Christ.

- Romans 3:23-24 (KJV): "For all have sinned, and come short of the glory of God; Being justified freely by his grace through the redemption that is in Christ Jesus."

The Call to Ethical Living

Moral agency entails a call to ethical living, reflecting God's character and purposes. Believers are called to live lives of integrity, justice, and compassion.

- Micah 6:8 (KJV): "He hath shewed thee, O man, what is good; and what doth the LORD require of thee, but to do justly, and to love mercy, and to walk humbly with thy God?"

Practical Reflections on Moral Agency

Cultivating a Sensitive Conscience

Believers are encouraged to cultivate a sensitive conscience, attuned to God's moral law and guided by the Holy Spirit.

- 1 Timothy 1:5 (KJV): "Now the end of the commandment is charity out of a pure heart, and of a good conscience, and of faith unfeigned."

Living with Integrity

Moral agency calls for living with integrity, making choices that are consistent with one's beliefs and values.

- Proverbs 11:3 (KJV): "The integrity of the upright shall guide them: but the perverseness of transgressors shall destroy them."

Seeking Forgiveness and Reconciliation

When moral failures occur, accountability involves seeking forgiveness and reconciliation with God and others.

- 1 John 1:9 (KJV): "If we confess our sins, he is faithful and just to forgive us our sins, and to cleanse us from all unrighteousness."

Promoting Justice and Compassion

Moral agency extends to promoting justice and compassion within society, advocating for the vulnerable and working towards the common good.

- Isaiah 1:17 (KJV): "Learn to do well; seek judgment, relieve the oppressed, judge the fatherless, plead for the widow."

Expository Study with Strong's Concordance

Conscience ("συνείδησις" syneidēsis)

The Greek word "συνείδησις" (syneidēsis), Strong's G4893, means conscience or moral consciousness. It refers to the inner sense of right and wrong that guides moral decisions.

- Romans 2:15 (KJV): "Which shew the work of the law written in their hearts, their conscience also bearing witness, and their thoughts the mean while accusing or else excusing one another."

Accountability ("ἀποδίδωμι" apodidōmi)

The Greek word "ἀποδίδωμι" (apodidōmi), Strong's G591, means to give back, repay, or render. It highlights the concept of giving an account or facing the consequences of one's actions.

- Romans 14:12 (KJV): "So then every one of us shall give account of himself to God."

Comprehensive Commentary

Interpreting Moral Agency and Accountability

The concept of moral agency emphasizes the responsibility and dignity of human beings as free agents capable of making significant moral choices. Accountability underscores the seriousness of these choices and their consequences.

Balancing Free Will and Divine Guidance

While humans are endowed with free will, divine guidance through Scripture and the Holy Spirit is essential for making righteous decisions. This balance highlights the importance of reliance on God in ethical living.

The Role of Community in Moral Development

Moral agency and accountability are nurtured within the context of community. Mutual encouragement, accountability, and support are vital for ethical growth and moral integrity.

- Hebrews 10:24-25 (KJV): "And let us consider one another to provoke unto love and to good works: Not forsaking the assembling of ourselves together, as the manner of some is; but exhorting one another: and so much the more, as ye see the day approaching."

The concept of moral agency and accountability is central to understanding human responsibility in Christian theology. Humans, created in the image of God, are endowed with free will and the capacity for moral judgment. This entails both the privilege of making significant choices and the responsibility of facing their consequences. Understanding moral agency highlights the importance of ethical living, the need for redemption, and the call to promote justice and compassion. This chapter has provided a comprehensive exploration of moral agency and accountability, offering theological insights and practical reflections for the Christian life.

How Free Will Leads to Moral Responsibility

Free will is a cornerstone of human existence, allowing individuals to make choices that carry moral significance. The concept of free will is intimately connected to moral responsibility, as it grants humans the capacity to choose between right and wrong and to be held accountable for their actions. This chapter explores how free will leads to moral responsibility, examining biblical foundations, theological implications, and practical reflections.

The Concept of Free Will

Definition of Free Will

Free will refers to the ability of individuals to make choices that are not determined by prior causes or divine intervention. It encompasses the capacity for self-determination and moral agency.

- Genesis 2:16-17 (KJV): "And the LORD God commanded the man, saying, Of every tree of the garden thou mayest freely eat: But of the tree of the knowledge of good and evil, thou shalt not eat of it: for in the day that thou eatest thereof thou shalt surely die."

Biblical Foundations of Free Will

The Bible affirms the existence of free will, portraying humans as moral agents capable of making significant choices. This capacity is rooted in being created in the image of God.

- Genesis 1:26-27 (KJV): "And God said, Let us make man in our image, after our likeness: and let them have dominion over the fish of the sea, and over the fowl of the air, and over the cattle, and over all the earth, and over every creeping thing that creepeth upon the earth. So God created man in his own image, in the image of God created he him; male and female created he them."

The Relationship Between Free Will and Moral Responsibility

Moral Agency and Accountability

Free will is the basis for moral agency, which entails the ability to make ethical decisions and be held accountable for them. Without free will, moral responsibility would be meaningless.

- Deuteronomy 30:19-20 (KJV): "I call heaven and earth to record this day against you, that I have set before you life and death, blessing and cursing: therefore choose life, that both thou and thy seed may live: That thou mayest love the LORD thy God, and that thou mayest obey his voice, and that thou mayest cleave unto him: for he is thy life, and the length of thy days: that thou mayest dwell in the land which the LORD sware unto thy fathers, to Abraham, to Isaac, and to Jacob, to give them."

The Exercise of Free Will

The exercise of free will involves making choices that align with or deviate from God's will. These choices carry moral weight and have consequences.

- Joshua 24:15 (KJV): "And if it seem evil unto you to serve the LORD, choose you this day whom ye will serve; whether the gods which your fathers served that were on the other side of the flood, or the gods of the Amorites, in whose land ye dwell: but as for me and my house, we will serve the LORD."

Consequences of Moral Choices

The Bible teaches that moral choices have consequences, both in this life and the life to come. Individuals are responsible for their actions and must face the outcomes of their decisions.

- Galatians 6:7-8 (KJV): "Be not deceived; God is not mocked: for whatsoever a man soweth, that shall he also reap. For he that soweth to his flesh shall of the flesh reap corruption; but he that soweth to the Spirit shall of the Spirit reap life everlasting."

Theological Implications of Free Will and Moral Responsibility

The Nature of Sin and Redemption

Free will is central to understanding sin and redemption. Sin results from the misuse of free will, while redemption involves the restoration of right relationship with God through Christ.

- Romans 3:23-24 (KJV): "For all have sinned, and come short of the glory of God; Being justified freely by his grace through the redemption that is in Christ Jesus."

God's Justice and Human Accountability

God's justice requires that humans be held accountable for their choices. Free will ensures that individuals are responsible for their actions and deserving of praise or blame.

- Ecclesiastes 12:14 (KJV): "For God shall bring every work into judgment, with every secret thing, whether it be good, or whether it be evil."

The Role of Conscience and the Holy Spirit

The conscience and the Holy Spirit guide believers in making moral choices. Free will allows individuals to respond to this guidance, leading to ethical living.

- John 16:13 (KJV): "Howbeit when he, the Spirit of truth, is come, he will guide you into all truth: for he shall not speak of himself; but whatsoever he shall hear, that shall he speak: and he will shew you things to come."

Practical Reflections on Free Will and Moral Responsibility

Cultivating Ethical Decision-Making

Believers are called to cultivate ethical decision-making through prayer, study of Scripture, and seeking the guidance of the Holy Spirit.

- Psalm 119:105 (KJV): "Thy word is a lamp unto my feet, and a light unto my path."

Living with Integrity

Exercising free will responsibly involves living with integrity, making choices that reflect one's values and commitment to God.

- Proverbs 11:3 (KJV): "The integrity of the upright shall guide them: but the perverseness of transgressors shall destroy them."

Seeking Forgiveness and Restoration

When moral failures occur, free will allows individuals to seek forgiveness and restoration through repentance and faith in Christ.

- 1 John 1:9 (KJV): "If we confess our sins, he is faithful and just to forgive us our sins, and to cleanse us from all unrighteousness."

Promoting Justice and Compassion

Free will also involves a call to promote justice and compassion, advocating for the vulnerable and working towards the common good.

- Micah 6:8 (KJV): "He hath shewed thee, O man, what is good; and what doth the LORD require of thee, but to do justly, and to love mercy, and to walk humbly with thy God?"

Expository Study with Strong's Concordance

Free Will ("ἐλευθερία" eleutheria)

The Greek word "ἐλευθερία" (eleutheria), Strong's G1657, means liberty or freedom. It highlights the capacity to make choices that are not coerced.

- Galatians 5:13 (KJV): "For, brethren, ye have been called unto liberty; only use not liberty for an occasion to the flesh, but by love serve one another."

Responsibility ("λογίζομαι" logizomai)

The Greek word "λογίζομαι" (logizomai), Strong's G3049, means to account or reckon. It underscores the idea of being held accountable for one's actions.

- Romans 14:12 (KJV): "So then every one of us shall give account of himself to God."

Comprehensive Commentary

Interpreting Free Will and Moral Responsibility

Free will is integral to the concept of moral responsibility. It grants individuals the capacity to make meaningful choices and be held accountable for them. This understanding is essential for grasping the nature of sin, redemption, and ethical living.

Balancing Freedom and Accountability

The exercise of free will must be balanced with a sense of accountability. Believers are called to use their freedom responsibly, making choices that honor God and reflect His character.

The Role of Community in Moral Development

Moral responsibility is nurtured within the context of community. Mutual encouragement, accountability, and support are vital for ethical growth and integrity.

- Hebrews 10:24-25 (KJV): "And let us consider one another to provoke unto love and to good works: Not forsaking the assembling of ourselves together, as the manner of some is; but exhorting one another: and so much the more, as ye see the day approaching."

Free will is a foundational aspect of human existence, granting individuals the capacity to make choices that carry moral significance. This chapter has explored how free will leads to moral responsibility, emphasizing the importance of ethical decision-making, accountability, and the guidance of the Holy Spirit. Understanding this relationship is crucial for living a life that honors God and reflects His purposes.

Examples of Human Choices Leading to Good and Evil Outcomes

Human history and biblical narratives provide numerous examples of how individual choices can lead to either good or evil outcomes. These choices reflect the exercise of free will and underscore the importance of moral responsibility. This chapter explores various biblical and historical examples of human choices, examining their consequences and the lessons they offer for ethical living.

Choices Leading to Good Outcomes

Joseph's Forgiveness and Leadership

Joseph's decision to forgive his brothers and use his position of power to save his family during a famine is a profound example of a good outcome resulting from righteous choices.

- Genesis 50:20 (KJV): "But as for you, ye thought evil against me; but God meant it unto good, to bring to pass, as it is this day, to save much people alive."

Ruth's Loyalty and Faithfulness

Ruth's choice to remain loyal to her mother-in-law Naomi and her subsequent marriage to Boaz led to blessings for herself and her descendants, including being part of the lineage of King David and Jesus.

- Ruth 1:16 (KJV): "And Ruth said, Intreat me not to leave thee, or to return from following after thee: for whither thou goest, I will go; and where thou lodgest, I will lodge: thy people shall be my people, and thy God my God."

Daniel's Integrity and Faithfulness

Daniel's decision to remain faithful to God, even in the face of potential death, resulted in his protection and elevation in the Babylonian and Persian empires.

- Daniel 6:22 (KJV): "My God hath sent his angel, and hath shut the lions' mouths, that they have not hurt me: forasmuch as before him innocency was found in me; and also before thee, O king, have I done no hurt."

Mary's Acceptance of God's Plan

Mary's willingness to accept God's plan for her to bear the Messiah brought about the fulfillment of God's promise of salvation.

- Luke 1:38 (KJV): "And Mary said, Behold the handmaid of the Lord; be it unto me according to thy word. And the angel departed from her."

The Good Samaritan's Compassion

The parable of the Good Samaritan illustrates the positive impact of choosing compassion and mercy over indifference.

- Luke 10:33-34 (KJV): "But a certain Samaritan, as he journeyed, came where he was: and when he saw him, he had compassion on him, And went to him, and bound up his wounds, pouring in oil and wine, and set him on his own beast, and brought him to an inn, and took care of him."

Choices Leading to Evil Outcomes

Adam and Eve's Disobedience

The decision of Adam and Eve to eat the forbidden fruit resulted in the fall of humanity, bringing sin and death into the world.

- Genesis 3:6 (KJV): "And when the woman saw that the tree was good for food, and that it was pleasant to the eyes, and a tree to be desired to make one wise, she took of the fruit thereof, and did eat, and gave also unto her husband with her; and he did eat."

Cain's Jealousy and Murder

Cain's choice to murder his brother Abel out of jealousy led to a curse on Cain and his descendants.

- Genesis 4:8-10 (KJV): "And Cain talked with Abel his brother: and it came to pass, when they were in the field, that Cain rose up against Abel his brother, and slew him. And the LORD said unto Cain, Where is Abel thy brother? And he said, I know not: Am I my brother's keeper? And he said,

What hast thou done? the voice of thy brother's blood crieth unto me from the ground."

David's Adultery and Murder

King David's decisions to commit adultery with Bathsheba and orchestrate the death of her husband Uriah brought severe consequences, including turmoil within his family and the loss of his child.

- 2 Samuel 11:4, 14-15 (KJV): "And David sent messengers, and took her; and she came in unto him, and he lay with her... And it came to pass in the morning, that David wrote a letter to Joab, and sent it by the hand of Uriah. And he wrote in the letter, saying, Set ye Uriah in the forefront of the hottest battle, and retire ye from him, that he may be smitten, and die."

Judas' Betrayal

Judas Iscariot's choice to betray Jesus for thirty pieces of silver led to his own demise and the crucifixion of Christ.

- Matthew 26:14-16 (KJV): "Then one of the twelve, called Judas Iscariot, went unto the chief priests, And said unto them, What will ye give me, and I will deliver him unto you? And they covenanted with him for thirty pieces of silver. And from that time he sought opportunity to betray him."

Ananias and Sapphira's Deceit

The decision of Ananias and Sapphira to lie about their donation to the early church resulted in their sudden deaths as a divine judgment.

- Acts 5:1-5 (KJV): "But a certain man named Ananias, with Sapphira his wife, sold a possession, And kept back part of the price, his wife also being privy to it, and brought a certain part, and laid it at the apostles' feet. But Peter said, Ananias, why hath Satan filled thine heart to lie to the Holy Ghost, and to keep back part of the price of the land?... And Ananias hearing these words fell down, and gave up the ghost: and great fear came on all them that heard these things."

Theological Implications of Human Choices

The Power of Free Will

Human choices demonstrate the power and responsibility of free will. The ability to choose between good and evil underscores the moral agency of individuals.

- Deuteronomy 30:19-20 (KJV): "I call heaven and earth to record this day against you, that I have set before you life and death, blessing and cursing: therefore choose life, that both thou and thy seed may live: That thou mayest love the LORD thy God, and that thou mayest obey his voice, and that thou mayest cleave unto him: for he is thy life, and the length of thy days: that thou mayest dwell in the land which the

LORD sware unto thy fathers, to Abraham, to Isaac, and to Jacob, to give them."

The Role of Divine Guidance

God provides guidance through Scripture, the Holy Spirit, and the community of faith to help individuals make righteous choices. Free will exercised in alignment with divine guidance leads to blessings.

- Psalm 119:105 (KJV): "Thy word is a lamp unto my feet, and a light unto my path."

Consequences of Sin and Obedience

The examples of human choices illustrate that sin leads to negative consequences, while obedience to God results in blessings and positive outcomes.

- Galatians 6:7-8 (KJV): "Be not deceived; God is not mocked: for whatsoever a man soweth, that shall he also reap. For he that soweth to his flesh shall of the flesh reap corruption; but he that soweth to the Spirit shall of the Spirit reap life everlasting."

Practical Reflections on Human Choices

Cultivating Righteous Decision-Making

Believers are called to cultivate righteous decision-making through prayer, studying Scripture, and seeking godly counsel.

- Proverbs 3:5-6 (KJV): "Trust in the LORD with all thine heart; and lean not unto thine own understanding. In all thy ways acknowledge him, and he shall direct thy paths."

Seeking Forgiveness and Restoration

When wrong choices are made, repentance and seeking God's forgiveness are essential for restoration and renewal.

- 1 John 1:9 (KJV): "If we confess our sins, he is faithful and just to forgive us our sins, and to cleanse us from all unrighteousness."

Promoting Justice and Compassion

Choosing to act justly and compassionately reflects God's character and advances His kingdom on earth.

- Micah 6:8 (KJV): "He hath shewed thee, O man, what is good; and what doth the LORD require of thee, but to do justly, and to love mercy, and to walk humbly with thy God?"

Living with Integrity

Integrity in decision-making involves consistency between one's values and actions, fostering trust and credibility.

- Proverbs 11:3 (KJV): "The integrity of the upright shall guide them: but the perverseness of transgressors shall destroy them."

Expository Study with Strong's Concordance

Choice ("בָּחַר" bachar)

The Hebrew word "בָּחַר" (bachar), Strong's H977, means to choose, select, or elect. It underscores the significance of making deliberate decisions.

- Joshua 24:15 (KJV): "And if it seem evil unto you to serve the LORD, choose you this day whom ye will serve; whether the gods which your fathers served that were on the other side of the flood, or the gods of the Amorites, in whose land ye dwell: but as for me and my house, we will serve the LORD."

Responsibility ("ἀποδίδωμι" apodidōmi)

The Greek word "ἀποδίδωμι" (apodidōmi), Strong's G591, means to give back, repay, or render. It highlights the concept of being accountable for one's actions.

- Romans 14:12 (KJV): "So then every one of us shall give account of himself to God."

Comprehensive Commentary

Interpreting Human Choices and Their Outcomes

Human choices reflect the exercise of free will and moral responsibility. Examples from biblical narratives illustrate the profound impact of decisions, both for good and evil.

The Balance of Freedom and Accountability

Free will must be exercised with a sense of accountability. Believers are called to make choices that honor God and reflect His character, knowing that their actions have significant consequences.

The Role of Divine Guidance in Ethical Living

God's guidance is essential for making righteous choices. Scripture, the Holy Spirit, and the faith community provide the wisdom and support needed for ethical decision-making.

Hope and Redemption in the Face of Wrong Choices

Even when wrong choices are made, the possibility of repentance and redemption offers hope. God's grace provides a path to restoration and renewal.

Human choices have the power to lead to both good and evil outcomes, reflecting the exercise of free will and moral responsibility. Biblical examples illustrate the profound impact of decisions and underscore the importance of aligning one's choices with God's will. This chapter has provided a comprehensive exploration of how human choices lead to different outcomes, offering theological insights and practical reflections for ethical living.

CHAPTER 08

SUFFERING AND GOD'S PLAN

The Problem of Suffering: Why Does a Good God Allow Pain?

The existence of suffering and pain in the world presents one of the most profound challenges to faith and theology. For many, the question arises: why does a good and loving God allow suffering? This chapter explores the problem of suffering, examining biblical perspectives, theological insights, and the broader context of God's plan. Understanding suffering in light of God's character and purposes can provide comfort and clarity for believers navigating the complexities of pain and adversity.

The Reality of Suffering

The Universality of Suffering

Suffering is a universal human experience that affects individuals and communities in various forms, including physical pain, emotional distress, and existential anguish.

- Job 5:7 (KJV): "Yet man is born unto trouble, as the sparks fly upward."

Biblical Examples of Suffering

The Bible provides numerous examples of suffering, from the trials of Job and the hardships of the Israelites to the persecution of the early Christians and the suffering of Jesus.

- Job 1:20-22 (KJV): "Then Job arose, and rent his mantle, and shaved his head, and fell down upon the ground, and worshipped, And said, Naked came I out of my mother's womb, and naked shall I return thither: the LORD gave, and the LORD hath taken away; blessed be the name of the LORD. In all this Job sinned not, nor charged God foolishly."

The Emotional and Spiritual Impact of Suffering

Suffering can lead to deep emotional and spiritual struggles, including feelings of abandonment, doubt, and questioning of God's goodness and justice.

- Psalm 22:1 (KJV): "My God, my God, why hast thou forsaken me? why art thou so far from helping me, and from the words of my roaring?"

Theological Perspectives on Suffering

The Problem of Evil and Theodicy

Theodicy is the theological attempt to justify God's goodness and omnipotence in the face of evil and suffering. Various approaches address this issue, including the free will defense, soul-making theodicy, and redemptive suffering.

- Romans 8:18 (KJV): "For I reckon that the sufferings of this present time are not worthy to be compared with the glory which shall be revealed in us."

Free Will and the Consequences of Sin

One explanation for suffering is the misuse of free will, leading to sin and its consequences. Human rebellion against God introduced moral and natural evil into the world.

- Genesis 3:16-19 (KJV): "Unto the woman he said, I will greatly multiply thy sorrow and thy conception; in sorrow thou shalt bring forth children; and thy desire shall be to thy husband, and he shall rule over thee. And unto Adam he said, Because thou hast hearkened unto the voice of thy wife, and hast eaten of the tree, of which I commanded thee, saying, Thou shalt not eat of it: cursed is the ground for thy sake; in sorrow shalt thou eat of it all the days of thy life; Thorns also and thistles shall it bring forth to thee; and thou shalt eat the herb of the field; In the sweat of thy face shalt thou eat bread, till thou return unto the ground; for out of it wast thou taken: for dust thou art, and unto dust shalt thou return."

Suffering as a Test of Faith

The Bible often portrays suffering as a test of faith, intended to strengthen and purify believers. Trials and tribulations can deepen trust in God and refine character.

- James 1:2-4 (KJV): "My brethren, count it all joy when ye fall into divers temptations; Knowing this, that the trying of your faith worketh patience. But let patience have her perfect work, that ye may be perfect and entire, wanting nothing."

Redemptive Suffering

Suffering can have redemptive purposes, both in the life of the sufferer and in the broader plan of God. Jesus' suffering and death on the cross serve as the ultimate example of redemptive suffering.

- 1 Peter 3:18 (KJV): "For Christ also hath once suffered for sins, the just for the unjust, that he might bring us to God, being put to death in the flesh, but quickened by the Spirit."

God's Plan and Purpose in Suffering

The Sovereignty of God

God's sovereignty means that He is in control of all things, including suffering. While we may not understand His purposes fully, we can trust that He is working all things for good.

- Romans 8:28 (KJV): "And we know that all things work together for good to them that love God, to them who are the called according to his purpose."

The Mystery of Suffering

Some aspects of suffering remain a mystery. The book of Job highlights that humans may not always comprehend God's reasons, but they are called to trust in His wisdom and goodness.

- Job 38:1-4 (KJV): "Then the LORD answered Job out of the whirlwind, and said, Who is this that darkeneth counsel by words without knowledge? Gird up now thy loins like a man; for I will demand of thee, and answer thou me. Where wast thou when I laid the foundations of the earth? declare, if thou hast understanding."

Suffering and Spiritual Growth

Suffering can lead to spiritual growth and maturity. It can drive individuals to seek God more earnestly and rely on His strength.

- Romans 5:3-5 (KJV): "And not only so, but we glory in tribulations also: knowing that tribulation worketh patience; And patience, experience; and experience, hope: And hope maketh not ashamed; because the love of God is shed abroad in our hearts by the Holy Ghost which is given unto us."

Comfort in Suffering

God provides comfort and presence in the midst of suffering. The Holy Spirit, described as the Comforter, offers peace and assurance to believers.

- 2 Corinthians 1:3-4 (KJV): "Blessed be God, even the Father of our Lord Jesus Christ, the Father of mercies, and the God of all comfort; Who comforteth us in all our tribulation, that we may be able to comfort them which are in any trouble, by the comfort wherewith we ourselves are comforted of God."

Practical Reflections on Suffering

Responding to Suffering with Faith

Believers are called to respond to suffering with faith, trusting in God's sovereignty and goodness even when circumstances are difficult.

- Habakkuk 3:17-19 (KJV): "Although the fig tree shall not blossom, neither shall fruit be in the vines; the labour of the olive shall fail, and the fields shall yield no meat; the flock shall be cut off from the fold, and there shall be no herd in the stalls: Yet I will rejoice in the LORD, I will joy in the God of my salvation. The LORD God is my strength, and he will make my feet like hinds' feet, and he will make me to walk upon mine high places."

Providing Compassion and Support

Christians are called to provide compassion and support to those who are suffering. Bearing one another's burdens is an essential aspect of living out the faith.

- Galatians 6:2 (KJV): "Bear ye one another's burdens, and so fulfil the law of Christ."

Seeking God in Suffering

Suffering can be a catalyst for deeper intimacy with God. In times of pain, individuals are encouraged to seek God through prayer, Scripture, and community.

- Psalm 34:18 (KJV): "The LORD is nigh unto them that are of a broken heart; and saveth such as be of a contrite spirit."

Hope and Eternal Perspective

Christians find hope in the promise of eternal life, where there will be no more suffering or pain. This eternal perspective provides strength and encouragement in the face of present trials.

- Revelation 21:4 (KJV): "And God shall wipe away all tears from their eyes; and there shall be no more death, neither sorrow, nor crying, neither shall there be any more pain: for the former things are passed away."

Expository Study with Strong's Concordance

Suffering ("πάσχω" pascho)

The Greek word "πάσχω" (pascho), Strong's G3958, means to suffer or undergo hardship. It reflects the experience of enduring pain and adversity.

- 1 Peter 4:19 (KJV): "Wherefore let them that suffer according to the will of God commit the keeping of their souls to him in well doing, as unto a faithful Creator."

Comfort ("παράκλησις" paraklesis)

The Greek word "παράκλησις" (paraklesis), Strong's G3874, means comfort, encouragement, or consolation. It highlights the role of the Holy Spirit and the community in providing support.

- 2 Corinthians 1:3-4 (KJV): "Blessed be God, even the Father of our Lord Jesus Christ, the Father of mercies, and the God of all comfort; Who comforteth us in all our tribulation, that we may be able to comfort them which are in any trouble, by the comfort wherewith we ourselves are comforted of God."

Comprehensive Commentary

Interpreting the Problem of Suffering

The problem of suffering is complex and multifaceted. It challenges believers to reconcile the existence of pain with the goodness and omnipotence of God. Various theological perspectives offer insights into this issue, emphasizing free will, the consequences of sin, and the redemptive purposes of suffering.

Balancing Trust and Understanding

While not all aspects of suffering can be fully understood, believers are called to trust in God's wisdom and sovereignty. Faith involves trusting God's character and promises even when circumstances are difficult.

The Role of Community in Suffering

The Christian community plays a vital role in supporting those who suffer. Mutual compassion, encouragement, and practical help reflect God's love and care.

Hope in Redemption and Restoration

The ultimate hope for believers lies in the promise of redemption and restoration. The suffering of this present time is temporary, and the assurance of eternal life provides comfort and strength.

The problem of suffering presents a profound challenge to faith, yet it also offers an opportunity to deepen trust in God's sovereignty and goodness. While the reasons for suffering may not always be clear, the Bible provides insights into its purpose and the assurance of God's presence and comfort. This chapter has explored the problem of suffering, offering theological perspectives and practical reflections to help believers navigate the complexities of pain and adversity.

Biblical Perspectives on Suffering and Trials

Suffering and trials are inevitable aspects of the human experience, and the Bible offers profound insights into their purpose and meaning. Understanding biblical perspectives on suffering can provide comfort, guidance, and hope for believers facing various hardships. This chapter explores how the Bible addresses suffering and trials, examining key passages and theological themes that illuminate God's purposes in the midst of adversity.

The Purpose of Suffering and Trials

Refinement and Growth

The Bible teaches that suffering and trials serve to refine and grow believers in their faith, character, and reliance on God.

- James 1:2-4 (KJV): "My brethren, count it all joy when ye fall into divers temptations; Knowing this, that the trying of your faith worketh patience. But let patience have her perfect work, that ye may be perfect and entire, wanting nothing."

- 1 Peter 1:6-7 (KJV): "Wherein ye greatly rejoice, though now for a season, if need be, ye are in heaviness through manifold temptations: That the trial of your faith, being much more precious than of gold that perisheth, though it be tried with fire, might be found unto praise and honour and glory at the appearing of Jesus Christ."

Discipline and Correction

Suffering can also be a form of divine discipline, intended to correct and guide believers back to righteous living.

- Hebrews 12:5-11 (KJV): "And ye have forgotten the exhortation which speaketh unto you as unto children, My son, despise not thou the chastening of the Lord, nor faint when thou art rebuked of him: For whom the Lord loveth he chasteneth, and scourgeth every son whom he receiveth... Now no chastening for the present seemeth to be joyous, but grievous: nevertheless afterward it yieldeth the peaceable fruit of righteousness unto them which are exercised thereby."

Identification with Christ

Suffering allows believers to share in the experiences of Christ, fostering a deeper union with Him and a better understanding of His sacrifice.

- Philippians 3:10 (KJV): "That I may know him, and the power of his resurrection, and the fellowship of his sufferings, being made conformable unto his death."

- 2 Corinthians 1:5 (KJV): "For as the sufferings of Christ abound in us, so our consolation also aboundeth by Christ."

Biblical Examples of Suffering and Trials

Job: The Paradigm of Suffering

Job's story is a profound exploration of human suffering and divine sovereignty. Despite intense personal loss and physical pain, Job maintains his faith, ultimately leading to restoration.

- Job 1:21-22 (KJV): "And said, Naked came I out of my mother's womb, and naked shall I return thither: the LORD gave, and the LORD hath taken away; blessed be the name of the LORD. In all this Job sinned not, nor charged God foolishly."

- Job 42:10 (KJV): "And the LORD turned the captivity of Job, when he prayed for his friends: also the LORD gave Job twice as much as he had before."

Joseph: From Betrayal to Blessing

Joseph's life, marked by betrayal, slavery, and imprisonment, illustrates how God can bring good out of suffering and trials.

- Genesis 50:20 (KJV): "But as for you, ye thought evil against me; but God meant it unto good, to bring to pass, as it is this day, to save much people alive."

Paul: Joy in Persecution

The Apostle Paul experienced extensive suffering, including imprisonment, beatings, and shipwrecks. His writings emphasize rejoicing in trials and finding strength in Christ.

- 2 Corinthians 12:9-10 (KJV): "And he said unto me, My grace is sufficient for thee: for my strength is made perfect in weakness. Most gladly therefore will I rather glory in my infirmities, that the power of Christ may rest upon me. Therefore I take pleasure in infirmities, in reproaches, in necessities, in persecutions, in distresses for Christ's sake: for when I am weak, then am I strong."

- Philippians 4:11-13 (KJV): "Not that I speak in respect of want: for I have learned, in whatsoever state I am, therewith to be content. I know both how to be abased, and I know how to abound: every where and in all things I am instructed both to be full and to be hungry, both to abound and to suffer need. I can do all things through Christ which strengtheneth me."

Theological Themes in Suffering

God's Sovereignty and Goodness

The Bible affirms that God is sovereign over all circumstances, including suffering. His plans are ultimately for the good of those who love Him, even when the immediate situation appears dire.

- Romans 8:28 (KJV): "And we know that all things work together for good to them that love God, to them who are the called according to his purpose."

The Mystery of Suffering

There are aspects of suffering that remain a mystery. The book of Job highlights that humans may not always understand God's reasons, but they are called to trust in His wisdom and goodness.

- Job 38:1-4 (KJV): "Then the LORD answered Job out of the whirlwind, and said, Who is this that darkeneth counsel by words without knowledge? Gird up now thy loins like a man; for I will demand of thee, and answer thou me. Where wast thou when I laid the foundations of the earth? declare, if thou hast understanding."

The Role of Faith and Perseverance

Faith and perseverance are essential in the face of suffering. Believers are encouraged to remain steadfast and trust in God's promises.

- Hebrews 10:36 (KJV): "For ye have need of patience, that, after ye have done the will of God, ye might receive the promise."

Comfort and Hope in Christ

Christ's presence provides comfort and hope amid suffering. The Holy Spirit, described as the Comforter, offers peace and assurance to believers.

- 2 Corinthians 1:3-5 (KJV): "Blessed be God, even the Father of our Lord Jesus Christ, the Father of mercies, and the God of all comfort; Who comforteth us in all our tribulation, that we may be able to comfort them which are in any trouble, by the comfort wherewith we ourselves are comforted of God. For as the sufferings of Christ abound in us, so our consolation also aboundeth by Christ."

Practical Reflections on Suffering and Trials

Responding with Faith

Believers are called to respond to suffering with faith, trusting in God's sovereignty and goodness even when circumstances are difficult.

- Habakkuk 3:17-19 (KJV): "Although the fig tree shall not blossom, neither shall fruit be in the vines; the labour of the olive shall fail, and the fields shall yield no meat; the flock shall be cut off from the fold, and there shall be no herd in the stalls: Yet I will rejoice in the LORD, I will joy in the God of my salvation. The LORD God is my strength, and he will make my feet like hinds' feet, and he will make me to walk upon mine high places."

Seeking God's Presence

In times of suffering, seeking God's presence through prayer, worship, and Scripture can provide strength and comfort.

- Psalm 34:18 (KJV): "The LORD is nigh unto them that are of a broken heart; and saveth such as be of a contrite spirit."

Community Support

The support of a faith community is vital during trials. Believers are encouraged to bear one another's burdens and provide practical help and encouragement.

- Galatians 6:2 (KJV): "Bear ye one another's burdens, and so fulfil the law of Christ."

Looking to Eternal Hope

Christians find hope in the promise of eternal life, where there will be no more suffering or pain. This eternal perspective provides strength and encouragement in the face of present trials.

- Revelation 21:4 (KJV): "And God shall wipe away all tears from their eyes; and there shall be no more death, neither sorrow, nor crying, neither shall there be any more pain: for the former things are passed away."

Expository Study with Strong's Concordance

Suffering ("πάσχω" pascho)

The Greek word "πάσχω" (pascho), Strong's G3958, means to suffer or undergo hardship. It reflects the experience of enduring pain and adversity.

- 1 Peter 4:19 (KJV): "Wherefore let them that suffer according to the will of God commit the keeping of their souls to him in well doing, as unto a faithful Creator."

Trial ("πειρασμός" peirasmos)

The Greek word "πειρασμός" (peirasmos), Strong's G3986, means trial, temptation, or testing. It emphasizes the challenges that test faith and character.

- James 1:2-3 (KJV): "My brethren, count it all joy when ye fall into divers temptations; Knowing this, that the trying of your faith worketh patience."

Comprehensive Commentary

Interpreting Biblical Perspectives on Suffering

The Bible provides a multifaceted understanding of suffering, viewing it as a tool for refinement, discipline, and deeper union with

Christ. These perspectives offer a framework for interpreting and responding to trials.

Balancing Trust and Understanding

While not all suffering can be fully understood, believers are called to trust in God's wisdom and sovereignty.

Faith involves trusting God's character and promises even when circumstances are difficult.

The Role of Community in Suffering

The Christian community plays a vital role in supporting those who suffer. Mutual compassion, encouragement, and practical help reflect God's love and care.

Hope and Redemption in the Face of Suffering

The ultimate hope for believers lies in the promise of redemption and restoration. The suffering of this present time is temporary, and the assurance of eternal life provides comfort and strength.

The Bible offers profound insights into the nature and purpose of suffering and trials. While suffering is an inevitable part of the human experience, it serves various divine purposes, including refinement, discipline, and identification with Christ. Understanding these biblical perspectives can provide comfort, guidance, and hope for believers navigating the complexities of pain and adversity. This chapter has explored the biblical perspectives on suffering, offering theological insights and practical reflections to help believers trust in God's plan and find strength in their faith.

Stories of Suffering in the Bible and Their Purposes

The Bible contains numerous accounts of suffering, each revealing different aspects of God's purposes and the human condition. These stories provide valuable lessons and insights into how God uses suffering for growth, refinement, and the fulfillment of His divine plan. This chapter explores several key biblical stories of suffering, examining their purposes and the lessons they offer for believers today.

Job: The Paradigm of Righteous Suffering

The Story of Job

Job is perhaps the most well-known biblical figure associated with suffering. A righteous man, Job faces immense loss and physical affliction, yet he remains faithful to God.

- Job 1:1-3 (KJV): "There was a man in the land of Uz, whose name was Job; and that man was perfect and upright, and one that feared God, and eschewed evil. And there were born unto him seven sons and three daughters. His substance also was seven thousand sheep, and three thousand camels, and five hundred yoke of oxen, and five hundred she asses, and a very great household; so that this man was the greatest of all the men of the east."

Purpose of Job's Suffering

Job's suffering serves multiple purposes:

1. Testing and Proving Faith: Job's faith is tested, proving his righteousness and integrity before God and man.

- Job 1:22 (KJV): "In all this Job sinned not, nor charged God foolishly."

2. Refining Character: Job's character is refined through his trials, leading to a deeper understanding of God and himself.

- Job 42:5-6 (KJV): "I have heard of thee by the hearing of the ear: but now mine eye seeth thee. Wherefore I abhor myself, and repent in dust and ashes."

3. Demonstrating Divine Sovereignty: The story highlights God's sovereignty and the limitations of human understanding.

- Job 38:1-4 (KJV): "Then the LORD answered Job out of the whirlwind, and said, Who is this that darkeneth counsel by words without knowledge? Gird up now thy loins like a man; for I will demand of thee, and answer thou me. Where wast thou when I laid the foundations of the earth? declare, if thou hast understanding."

Joseph: Suffering and Divine Providence

The Story of Joseph

Joseph, sold into slavery by his brothers, faces numerous hardships, including false accusations and imprisonment. Despite these trials, he rises to a position of power in Egypt.

- Genesis 37:23-28 (KJV): "And it came to pass, when Joseph was come unto his brethren, that they stript Joseph out of his coat, his coat of many colours that was on him; And they took him, and cast him into a pit... And there passed by Midianites merchantmen; and they drew and lifted up Joseph out of the pit, and sold Joseph to the Ishmeelites for twenty pieces of silver: and they brought Joseph into Egypt."

Purpose of Joseph's Suffering

Joseph's suffering serves to demonstrate God's providence and sovereign plan:

1. Preparation for Leadership: Joseph's trials prepare him for a significant leadership role in Egypt.

- Genesis 41:41 (KJV): "And Pharaoh said unto Joseph, See, I have set thee over all the land of Egypt."

2. Family Reconciliation: Joseph's position enables him to reconcile with his brothers and save his family from famine.

- Genesis 45:5 (KJV): "Now therefore be not grieved, nor angry with yourselves, that ye sold me hither: for God did send me before you to preserve life."

3. Fulfillment of God's Promises: Joseph's story illustrates the fulfillment of God's promises and His ability to bring good out of evil.

- Genesis 50:20 (KJV): "But as for you, ye thought evil against me; but God meant it unto good, to bring to pass, as it is this day, to save much people alive."

Naomi and Ruth: Suffering and Redemption

The Story of Naomi and Ruth

Naomi, after losing her husband and sons, returns to Bethlehem with her daughter-in-law Ruth. Ruth's loyalty and eventual marriage to Boaz lead to restoration and blessing.

- Ruth 1:16-17 (KJV): "And Ruth said, Intreat me not to leave thee, or to return from following after thee: for whither thou goest, I will go; and where thou lodgest, I will lodge: thy people shall be my people, and thy God my God: Where thou diest, will I die, and there will I be buried: the LORD do so to me, and more also, if ought but death part thee and me."

Purpose of Naomi and Ruth's Suffering

The suffering of Naomi and Ruth serves several purposes:

1. Demonstration of Loyalty and Faith: Ruth's loyalty to Naomi and faith in God are highlighted as exemplary virtues.

- Ruth 2:11-12 (KJV): "And Boaz answered and said unto her, It hath fully been shewed me, all that thou hast done unto thy mother in law since the death of thine husband: and how thou hast left thy father and thy mother, and the land of thy nativity, and art come unto a people which thou knewest not heretofore. The LORD recompense thy work, and a full reward be given thee of the LORD God of Israel, under whose wings thou art come to trust."

2. Providence and Redemption: Their story illustrates God's providence and the theme of redemption, culminating in the lineage of King David and ultimately Jesus.

- Ruth 4:13-17 (KJV): "So Boaz took Ruth, and she was his wife: and when he went in unto her, the LORD gave her conception, and she bare a son... And the women her neighbours gave it a name, saying, There is a son born to Naomi; and they called his name Obed: he is the father of Jesse, the father of David."

3. Transformation through Suffering: Naomi's journey from bitterness to joy demonstrates how God can transform suffering into blessing.

- Ruth 4:14-15 (KJV): "And the women said unto Naomi, Blessed be the LORD, which hath not left thee this day without a kinsman, that his name may be famous in Israel. And he shall be unto thee a restorer of thy life, and a nourisher of thine old age: for thy daughter in law, which loveth thee, which is better to thee than seven sons, hath born him."

David: Suffering and Leadership

The Story of David

David experiences significant suffering, including being pursued by King Saul, personal failures, and family strife. Despite these hardships, he remains a man after God's own heart.

- 1 Samuel 19:10 (KJV): "And Saul sought to smite David even to the wall with the javelin: but he slipped away out of Saul's presence, and he smote the javelin into the wall: and David fled, and escaped that night."

Purpose of David's Suffering

David's suffering serves to shape his character and leadership:

1. Development of Character: David's trials develop his character, making him a compassionate and humble leader.

- Psalm 51:17 (KJV): "The sacrifices of God are a broken spirit: a broken and a contrite heart, O God, thou wilt not despise."

2. Dependence on God: His suffering teaches him to rely on God's strength and guidance.

- Psalm 23:4 (KJV): "Yea, though I walk through the valley of the shadow of death, I will fear no evil: for thou art with me; thy rod and thy staff they comfort me."

3. Preparation for Kingship: The experiences prepare him to rule Israel with wisdom and justice.

- 2 Samuel 5:2-3 (KJV): "Also in time past, when Saul was king over us, thou wast he that leddest out and broughtest in Israel: and the LORD said to thee, Thou shalt feed my people Israel, and thou shalt be a captain over Israel. So all the elders of Israel came to the king to Hebron; and king David made a league with them in Hebron before the LORD: and they anointed David king over Israel."

Paul: Suffering and Mission

The Story of Paul

The Apostle Paul endures extensive suffering, including imprisonment, beatings, and shipwrecks, as he spreads the gospel across the Roman Empire.

- 2 Corinthians 11:24-27 (KJV): "Of the Jews five times received I forty stripes save one. Thrice was I beaten with rods, once was I stoned, thrice I suffered shipwreck, a night and a day I have been in the deep; In journeyings often, in perils of waters, in perils of robbers, in perils by mine own countrymen, in perils by the heathen, in perils in the city, in perils in the wilderness, in perils in the sea, in perils among false brethren; In weariness and painfulness, in watchings often, in hunger and thirst, in fastings often, in cold and nakedness."

Purpose of Paul's Suffering

Paul's suffering advances the mission of the gospel:

1. Strengthening the Church: His trials encourage and strengthen the early Christian communities.

- Philippians 1:12-14 (KJV): "But I would ye should understand, brethren, that the things which happened unto me have fallen out rather unto the furtherance of the gospel; So that my bonds in Christ are manifest in all the palace, and in all other places; And many of the brethren in the Lord, waxing confident by my bonds, are much more bold to speak the word without fear."

2. Demonstrating God's Power: Paul's endurance showcases God's power and grace at work in his life.

- 2 Corinthians 12:9 (KJV): "And he said unto me, My grace is sufficient for thee: for my strength is made perfect in weakness. Most gladly therefore will I rather glory in my infirmities, that the power of Christ may rest upon me."

3. Expanding the Gospel: His suffering facilitates the spread of the gospel to new regions and people.

- Acts 28:30-31 (KJV): "And Paul dwelt two whole years in his own hired house, and received all that came in unto him, Preaching the kingdom of God, and teaching those things which concern the Lord Jesus Christ, with all confidence, no man forbidding him."

Jesus: The Ultimate Suffering Servant

The Story of Jesus

Jesus' life and ministry culminate in His suffering and crucifixion, which are central to the Christian faith.

- Isaiah 53:3-5 (KJV): "He is despised and rejected of men; a man of sorrows, and acquainted with grief: and we hid as it were our faces from him; he was despised, and we esteemed him not. Surely he hath borne our griefs, and carried our sorrows: yet we did esteem him stricken, smitten of God, and afflicted. But he was wounded for our transgressions, he was bruised for our iniquities: the chastisement of our peace was upon him; and with his stripes we are healed."

Purpose of Jesus' Suffering

Jesus' suffering serves the highest divine purpose:

1. Atonement for Sin: His suffering and death atone for the sins of humanity, reconciling people to God.

- 1 Peter 3:18 (KJV): "For Christ also hath once suffered for sins, the just for the unjust, that he might bring us to God, being put to death in the flesh, but quickened by the Spirit."

2. Exemplifying Perfect Obedience: Jesus' willingness to suffer demonstrates perfect obedience to the Father.

- Philippians 2:8 (KJV): "And being found in fashion as a man, he humbled himself, and became obedient unto death, even the death of the cross."

3. Defeating Sin and Death: His resurrection signifies the ultimate victory over sin and death.

- 1 Corinthians 15:54-57 (KJV): "So when this corruptible shall have put on incorruption, and this mortal shall have put on immortality, then shall be brought to pass the saying that is written, Death is swallowed up in victory. O death, where is thy sting? O grave, where is thy victory? The sting of death is sin; and the strength of sin is the law. But thanks be to God, which giveth us the victory through our Lord Jesus Christ."

Practical Reflections on Suffering

Responding with Faith and Trust

Believers are encouraged to respond to suffering with faith and trust in God's sovereignty and goodness.

- James 1:2-4 (KJV): "My brethren, count it all joy when ye fall into divers temptations; Knowing this, that the trying of your faith worketh patience. But let patience have her perfect work, that ye may be perfect and entire, wanting nothing."

Seeking God in Suffering

Suffering can deepen one's relationship with God, driving individuals to seek Him more earnestly.

- Psalm 34:18 (KJV): "The LORD is nigh unto them that are of a broken heart; and saveth such as be of a contrite spirit."

Supporting Others in Their Trials

Christians are called to support and comfort those who are suffering, reflecting Christ's love and compassion.

- 2 Corinthians 1:3-4 (KJV): "Blessed be God, even the Father of our Lord Jesus Christ, the Father of mercies, and the God of all comfort; Who comforteth us in all our tribulation, that we may be able to comfort them which are in any trouble, by the comfort wherewith we ourselves are comforted of God."

Hope and Eternal Perspective

Believers find hope in the promise of eternal life, where suffering and pain will be no more.

- Revelation 21:4 (KJV): "And God shall wipe away all tears from their eyes; and there shall be no more death, neither sorrow, nor crying, neither shall there be any more pain: for the former things are passed away."

Expository Study with Strong's Concordance

Suffering ("πάσχω" pascho)

The Greek word "πάσχω" (pascho), Strong's G3958, means to suffer or undergo hardship. It reflects the experience of enduring pain and adversity.

1 Peter 4:19 (KJV): "Wherefore let them that suffer according to the will of God commit the keeping of their souls to him in well doing, as unto a faithful Creator."

Comfort ("παράκλησις" paraklesis)

The Greek word "παράκλησις" (paraklesis), Strong's G3874, means comfort, encouragement, or consolation. It highlights the role of the Holy Spirit and the community in providing support.

- 2 Corinthians 1:3-4 (KJV): "Blessed be God, even the Father of our Lord Jesus Christ, the Father of mercies, and the God of all comfort; Who comforteth us in all our tribulation, that we may be able to comfort them which are in any trouble, by the comfort wherewith we ourselves are comforted of God."

Comprehensive Commentary

Interpreting Stories of Suffering

Biblical stories of suffering reveal the multifaceted purposes of God in allowing trials. These stories teach valuable lessons about faith, perseverance, and the transformative power of God's grace.

Balancing Trust and Understanding

While not all suffering can be fully understood, believers are called to trust in God's wisdom and sovereignty. Faith involves trusting God's character and promises even when circumstances are difficult.

The Role of Community in Suffering

The Christian community plays a vital role in supporting those who suffer. Mutual compassion, encouragement, and practical help reflect God's love and care.

Hope and Redemption in the Face of Suffering

The ultimate hope for believers lies in the promise of redemption and restoration. The suffering of this present time is temporary, and the assurance of eternal life provides comfort and strength.

The Bible offers profound insights into the nature and purpose of suffering through the stories of various individuals. These accounts illustrate how God uses suffering to refine, correct, and fulfill His divine purposes. Understanding these stories can provide comfort, guidance, and hope for believers navigating the complexities of pain and adversity. This chapter has explored several key biblical stories of suffering, offering theological insights and practical reflections to help believers trust in God's plan and find strength in their faith.

This chapter has examined stories of suffering in the Bible and their purposes, laying the groundwork for further discussions on the nature of evil, the role of free will, and the redemptive purposes of God. The next chapters will build on these insights, delving deeper into the implications of suffering and the hope of redemption in the Christian life.

CHAPTER 09

REDEMPTION AND RESTORATION

God's Plan for Redemption Through Jesus Christ

Redemption and restoration are central themes in Christian theology, encapsulating God's plan to rescue humanity from sin and its consequences through Jesus Christ. This chapter explores the biblical foundation of redemption, the significance of Christ's sacrifice, and the transformative impact of God's redemptive work. Understanding these concepts is crucial for grasping the depth of God's love and the hope offered through Jesus Christ.

The Need for Redemption

The Fall and Human Sinfulness

The need for redemption arises from the fall of humanity. Adam and Eve's disobedience introduced sin into the world, resulting in separation from God and the need for salvation.

- Genesis 3:6-7 (KJV): "And when the woman saw that the tree was good for food, and that it was pleasant to the eyes, and a tree to be desired to make one wise, she took of the fruit thereof, and did eat, and gave also unto her husband with her; and he did eat. And the eyes of them both were opened, and they knew that they were naked; and they sewed fig leaves together, and made themselves aprons."

The Consequences of Sin

Sin brought about physical, spiritual, and relational brokenness, necessitating a divine solution to restore humanity to its intended state.

- Romans 3:23 (KJV): "For all have sinned, and come short of the glory of God."

- Romans 6:23 (KJV): "For the wages of sin is death; but the gift of God is eternal life through Jesus Christ our Lord."

God's Promise of Redemption

The Protoevangelium

The first hint of redemption appears in Genesis 3:15, known as the protoevangelium, where God promises a future Savior who will defeat the serpent.

- Genesis 3:15 (KJV): "And I will put enmity between thee and the woman, and between thy seed and her seed; it shall bruise thy head, and thou shalt bruise his heel."

Covenants and Prophecies

Throughout the Old Testament, God establishes covenants and provides prophecies pointing to the coming Messiah who will redeem His people.

- Genesis 12:3 (KJV): "And I will bless them that bless thee, and curse him that curseth thee: and in thee shall all families of the earth be blessed."

- Isaiah 53:5 (KJV): "But he was wounded for our transgressions, he was bruised for our iniquities: the chastisement of our peace was upon him; and with his stripes we are healed."

The Fulfillment of Redemption in Jesus Christ

The Incarnation

God's plan for redemption culminates in the incarnation of Jesus Christ, fully God and fully man, who enters the world to fulfill the promise of salvation.

- John 1:14 (KJV): "And the Word was made flesh, and dwelt among us, (and we beheld his glory, the glory as of the only begotten of the Father,) full of grace and truth."

The Sacrificial Death of Christ

The crucifixion of Jesus is the central act of redemption. Through His sacrificial death, He atones for the sins of humanity, satisfying divine justice and demonstrating God's love.

- 1 Peter 2:24 (KJV): "Who his own self bare our sins in his own body on the tree, that we, being dead to sins, should live unto righteousness: by whose stripes ye were healed."

- Romans 5:8 (KJV): "But God commendeth his love toward us, in that, while we were yet sinners, Christ died for us."

The Resurrection

The resurrection of Jesus from the dead confirms the efficacy of His sacrifice, conquering death and offering new life to all who believe.

- 1 Corinthians 15:3-4 (KJV): "For I delivered unto you first of all that which I also received, how that Christ died for our sins according to the scriptures; And that he was buried, and that he rose again the third day according to the scriptures."

- 1 Peter 1:3 (KJV): "Blessed be the God and Father of our Lord Jesus Christ, which according to his abundant mercy hath begotten us again unto a lively hope by the resurrection of Jesus Christ from the dead."

The Process of Redemption

Justification

Justification is the act of God declaring sinners righteous through faith in Jesus Christ. It is a legal standing before God, based on the righteousness of Christ imputed to believers.

- Romans 3:24 (KJV): "Being justified freely by his grace through the redemption that is in Christ Jesus."

- 2 Corinthians 5:21 (KJV): "For he hath made him to be sin for us, who knew no sin; that we might be made the righteousness of God in him."

Sanctification

Sanctification is the ongoing process of being made holy, involving the transformation of character and conduct through the work of the Holy Spirit.

- 1 Thessalonians 4:3 (KJV): "For this is the will of God, even your sanctification, that ye should abstain from fornication."

- Philippians 2:12-13 (KJV): "Wherefore, my beloved, as ye have always obeyed, not as in my presence only, but now much more in my absence, work out your own salvation with fear and trembling. For it is God which worketh in you both to will and to do of his good pleasure."

Glorification

Glorification is the future completion of redemption when believers are transformed into the likeness of Christ and dwell with God eternally.

- Romans 8:30 (KJV): "Moreover whom he did predestinate, them he also called: and whom he called, them he also justified: and whom he justified, them he also glorified."

- 1 John 3:2 (KJV): "Beloved, now are we the sons of God, and it doth not yet appear what we shall be: but we know that, when he shall appear, we shall be like him; for we shall see him as he is."

The Impact of Redemption

Reconciliation with God

Redemption restores the broken relationship between humanity and God, offering peace and fellowship through Jesus Christ.

- Colossians 1:20 (KJV): "And, having made peace through the blood of his cross, by him to reconcile all things unto himself; by him, I say, whether they be things in earth, or things in heaven."

- 2 Corinthians 5:18-19 (KJV): "And all things are of God, who hath reconciled us to himself by Jesus Christ, and hath given to us the ministry of reconciliation; To wit, that God was in Christ, reconciling the world unto himself, not imputing their trespasses unto them; and hath committed unto us the word of reconciliation."

Adoption into God's Family

Believers are adopted into God's family, becoming His children and heirs to His promises.

- Galatians 4:4-5 (KJV): "But when the fulness of the time was come, God sent forth his Son, made of a woman, made under the law, To redeem them that were under the law, that we might receive the adoption of sons."

- Romans 8:15-17 (KJV): "For ye have not received the spirit of bondage again to fear; but ye have received the Spirit of adoption, whereby we cry, Abba, Father. The Spirit itself beareth witness with our spirit, that we are the children of God: And if children, then heirs; heirs of God, and joint-heirs with Christ; if so be that we suffer with him, that we may be also glorified together."

Empowerment for Holy Living

Through redemption, believers receive the Holy Spirit, who empowers them to live holy lives and bear fruit for God's kingdom.

- Galatians 5:22-23 (KJV): "But the fruit of the Spirit is love, joy, peace, longsuffering, gentleness, goodness, faith, Meekness, temperance: against such there is no law."

- Acts 1:8 (KJV): "But ye shall receive power, after that the Holy Ghost is come upon you: and ye shall be witnesses unto me both in Jerusalem, and in all Judaea, and in Samaria, and unto the uttermost part of the earth."

Practical Reflections on Redemption

Living in Gratitude

Believers are called to live in gratitude for the gift of redemption, offering their lives as a response to God's grace.

- Romans 12:1 (KJV): "I beseech you therefore, brethren, by the mercies of God, that ye present your bodies a living sacrifice, holy, acceptable unto God, which is your reasonable service."

Sharing the Message of Redemption

The message of redemption through Jesus Christ is meant to be shared with others, fulfilling the Great Commission.

- Matthew 28:19-20 (KJV): "Go ye therefore, and teach all nations, baptizing them in the name of the Father, and of the Son, and of the Holy Ghost: Teaching them to observe all things whatsoever I have commanded you: and, lo, I am with you alway, even unto the end of the world. Amen."

Trusting in God's Promises

Believers are encouraged to trust in

God's promises, knowing that His plan of redemption will be fully realized.

- 2 Peter 3:13 (KJV): "Nevertheless we, according to his promise, look for new heavens and a new earth, wherein dwelleth righteousness."

Expository Study with Strong's Concordance

Redemption ("ἀπολύτρωσις" apolytrōsis)

The Greek word "ἀπολύτρωσις" (apolytrōsis), Strong's G629, means release or deliverance. It refers to the act of freeing someone from bondage or captivity, often at a great cost.

- Ephesians 1:7 (KJV): "In whom we have redemption through his blood, the forgiveness of sins, according to the riches of his grace."

Reconciliation ("καταλλαγή" katallagē)

The Greek word "καταλλαγή" (katallagē), Strong's G2643, means reconciliation or restoration of favor. It emphasizes the restoration of a relationship that has been broken.

- 2 Corinthians 5:18 (KJV): "And all things are of God, who hath reconciled us to himself by Jesus Christ, and hath given to us the ministry of reconciliation."

Comprehensive Commentary

Interpreting God's Plan for Redemption

God's plan for redemption through Jesus Christ is the fulfillment of His promise to restore humanity. It involves the sacrificial death and resurrection of Jesus, which atones for sin and brings new life to believers.

The Transformative Power of Redemption

Redemption transforms individuals, reconciling them to God, adopting them into His family, and empowering them to live holy lives. It is a comprehensive work that impacts every aspect of a believer's life.

Living Out the Implications of Redemption

Believers are called to live out the implications of redemption, responding with gratitude, sharing the message of salvation, and trusting in God's promises. The redeemed life is one of ongoing transformation and mission.

God's plan for redemption through Jesus Christ is the cornerstone of the Christian faith. It addresses the need for salvation, fulfills God's promises, and transforms believers. Understanding and embracing this plan provides hope, purpose, and direction for the Christian life. This chapter has explored the biblical foundation and practical implications of redemption, offering theological insights and reflections to help believers live out their faith.

The Role of Jesus in Addressing the Problem of Evil

The problem of evil has long been a central issue in theology and philosophy, questioning how a good and omnipotent God can allow the existence of evil and suffering in the world. Jesus Christ's life, death, and resurrection provide the definitive answer to this problem within Christian theology. This chapter explores the role of Jesus in addressing the problem of evil, examining His mission, actions, and the implications of His work for humanity and creation.

The Nature of Evil and Its Origins

The Introduction of Evil

Evil entered the world through the disobedience of Adam and Eve, resulting in the fall of humanity and the subsequent spread of sin and suffering.

- Genesis 3:1-7 (KJV): "Now the serpent was more subtil than any beast of the field which the LORD God had made. And he said unto the woman, Yea, hath God said, Ye shall not eat of every tree of the garden? And the woman said unto the serpent, We may eat of the fruit of the trees of the garden: But of the fruit of the tree which is in the midst of the garden, God hath said, Ye shall not eat of it, neither shall ye touch it, lest ye die. And the serpent said unto the woman, Ye shall not surely die: For God doth know that in the day ye eat thereof, then your eyes shall be opened, and ye shall be as gods, knowing good and evil. And when the woman saw that the tree was good for food, and that it was pleasant to the eyes, and a tree to be desired to make one wise, she took of the fruit thereof, and did eat, and gave also unto her husband with her; and he did eat. And the eyes of them both were opened, and they knew that they were naked; and they sewed fig leaves together, and made themselves aprons."

The Consequences of Evil

Sin brought about spiritual death, physical suffering, and separation from God. It corrupted the created order and introduced pain, conflict, and injustice.

- Romans 5:12 (KJV): "Wherefore, as by one man sin entered into the world, and death by sin; and so death passed upon all men, for that all have sinned."

The Mission of Jesus

The Incarnation

Jesus, the Son of God, took on human flesh to address the problem of evil directly. The incarnation signifies God's entry into the human condition to redeem and restore.

- John 1:14 (KJV): "And the Word was made flesh, and dwelt among us, (and we beheld his glory, the glory as of the only begotten of the Father,) full of grace and truth."

Preaching the Kingdom of God

Jesus proclaimed the arrival of God's kingdom, offering a vision of a restored world where evil and suffering are overcome by divine justice, mercy, and peace.

- Matthew 4:17 (KJV): "From that time Jesus began to preach, and to say, Repent: for the kingdom of heaven is at hand."

Healing and Deliverance

Jesus' miracles of healing and exorcism demonstrate His authority over evil, sickness, and demonic forces. These acts provide a foretaste of the complete eradication of evil.

- Matthew 8:16-17 (KJV): "When the even was come, they brought unto him many that were possessed with devils: and he cast out the spirits with his word, and healed all that were sick: That it might be fulfilled which was spoken by Esaias the prophet, saying, Himself took our infirmities, and bare our sicknesses."

The Crucifixion: Confronting Evil

The Atonement for Sin

Jesus' death on the cross addresses the root problem of evil—sin. By bearing the punishment for sin, Jesus provides atonement and reconciles humanity to God.

- 1 Peter 2:24 (KJV): "Who his own self bare our sins in his own body on the tree, that we, being dead to sins, should live unto righteousness: by whose stripes ye were healed."

Defeating the Powers of Evil

The crucifixion is also a cosmic victory over the powers of evil. Jesus' death disarms the principalities and powers, triumphing over them.

- Colossians 2:15 (KJV): "And having spoiled principalities and powers, he made a shew of them openly, triumphing over them in it."

Absorbing Suffering and Injustice

In His suffering, Jesus identifies with human pain and injustice, offering a profound example of redemptive suffering.

- Isaiah 53:3-5 (KJV): "He is despised and rejected of men; a man of sorrows, and acquainted with grief: and we hid as it were our faces from him; he was despised, and we esteemed him not. Surely he hath borne our griefs, and carried our sorrows: yet we did esteem him stricken, smitten of God, and afflicted. But he was wounded for our transgressions, he was bruised for our iniquities: the chastisement of our peace was upon him; and with his stripes we are healed."

The Resurrection: The Triumph Over Evil

The Victory Over Death

Jesus' resurrection is the definitive proof of His victory over sin and death. It inaugurates the new creation where death and suffering are ultimately defeated.

- 1 Corinthians 15:54-57 (KJV): "So when this corruptible shall have put on incorruption, and this mortal shall have put on immortality, then shall be brought to pass the saying that is written, Death is swallowed up in victory. O death, where is thy sting? O grave, where is thy victory? The sting of death is sin; and the strength of sin is the law. But thanks be to God, which giveth us the victory through our Lord Jesus Christ."

The Promise of Restoration

The resurrection assures believers of the future restoration of all things. It points to the time when evil will be completely eradicated, and God's perfect justice will prevail.

- Revelation 21:4 (KJV): "And God shall wipe away all tears from their eyes; and there shall be no more death, neither sorrow, nor crying, neither shall there be any more pain: for the former things are passed away."

Empowering Believers

The resurrection empowers believers with the Holy Spirit, enabling them to live victoriously over sin and participate in God's redemptive work.

- Romans 8:11 (KJV): "But if the Spirit of him that raised up Jesus from the dead dwell in you, he that raised up Christ from the dead shall also quicken your mortal bodies by his Spirit that dwelleth in you."

The Ongoing Role of Jesus in Addressing Evil

Intercession for Believers

Jesus continues to address the problem of evil through His role as an intercessor, advocating for believers before the Father.

- Hebrews 7:25 (KJV): "Wherefore he is able also to save them to the uttermost that come unto God by him, seeing he ever liveth to make intercession for them."

The Presence of the Holy Spirit

The Holy Spirit, sent by Jesus, empowers and guides believers in their struggle against evil, providing comfort and strength.

- John 14:16-17 (KJV): "And I will pray the Father, and he shall give you another Comforter, that he may abide with you for ever; Even the Spirit of truth; whom the world cannot receive, because it seeth him not, neither knoweth him: but ye know him; for he dwelleth with you, and shall be in you."

The Mission of the Church

The Church, as the body of Christ, is called to confront evil and injustice, embodying the values of the kingdom of God in the world.

- Matthew 16:18 (KJV): "And I say also unto thee, That thou art Peter, and upon this rock I will build my church; and the gates of hell shall not prevail against it."

Practical Reflections on Jesus' Role in Addressing Evil

Living in the Victory of Christ

Believers are called to live in the victory won by Christ, resisting evil and embodying the values of the kingdom of God.

- 1 John 5:4 (KJV): "For whatsoever is born of God overcometh the world: and this is the victory that overcometh the world, even our faith."

Engaging in Spiritual Warfare

Understanding Jesus' victory over evil equips believers to engage in spiritual warfare, standing firm against the forces of darkness.

- Ephesians 6:12-13 (KJV): "For we wrestle not against flesh and blood, but against principalities, against powers, against the rulers of the darkness of this world, against spiritual wickedness in high places. Wherefore take unto you the whole armour of God, that ye may be able to withstand in the evil day, and having done all, to stand."

Participating in God's Redemptive Work

Believers are invited to participate in God's redemptive work by promoting justice, mercy, and peace in their communities and the world.

- Micah 6:8 (KJV): "He hath shewed thee, O man, what is good; and what doth the LORD require of thee, but to do justly, and to love mercy, and to walk humbly with thy God?"

Expository Study with Strong's Concordance

Evil ("πονηρός" ponēros)

The Greek word "πονηρός" (ponēros), Strong's G4190, means evil, wicked, or malicious. It encompasses moral evil and the malevolent actions of individuals and spiritual forces.

- Matthew 6:13 (KJV): "And lead us not into temptation, but deliver us from evil: For thine is the kingdom, and the power, and the glory, for ever. Amen."

Redemption ("ἀπολύτρωσις" apolytrōsis)

The Greek word "ἀπολύτρωσις" (apolytrōsis), Strong's G629, means release or deliverance. It refers to the act of freeing someone from bondage or captivity, often at a great cost.

- Ephesians 1:7 (KJV): "In whom we have redemption through his blood, the forgiveness of sins, according to the riches of his grace."

Comprehensive Commentary

Interpreting Jesus' Role in Addressing Evil

Jesus' life, death, and resurrection provide a comprehensive solution to the problem of evil. His work addresses the root causes of sin and offers a path to restoration and redemption.

The Transformative Power of Jesus' Victory

Jesus' victory over evil transforms individuals and communities, offering hope and the promise of a future free from suffering and injustice. Believers are called to live out this victory in their daily lives.

The Ongoing Mission of the Church

The Church, empowered by the Holy Spirit, continues Jesus' mission of confronting evil and promoting God's kingdom. This involves spiritual warfare, acts of justice and mercy, and the proclamation of the gospel.

Jesus Christ plays a central role in addressing the problem of evil, offering a definitive solution through His life, death, and resurrection. His victory over sin and death provides hope, restoration, and the promise of a future free from evil and suffering. This chapter has explored the multifaceted role of Jesus in confronting evil, offering theological insights and practical reflections to help believers live in the victory of Christ and participate in God's redemptive work.

The Promise of a Restored Creation and the End of Evil

The Christian hope is rooted in the promise of a restored creation where evil and suffering are no more. This hope is woven throughout the biblical narrative, culminating in the vision of a new heaven and a new earth. This chapter explores the biblical promise of restoration, the defeat of evil, and the ultimate renewal of all things through Jesus Christ. Understanding these promises provides believers with hope and encouragement as they navigate the present world.

The Biblical Foundation of Restoration

The Promise of Redemption in Genesis

The promise of restoration begins with the protoevangelium in Genesis, where God declares His plan to defeat evil and redeem humanity.

- Genesis 3:15 (KJV): "And I will put enmity between thee and the woman, and between thy seed and her seed; it shall bruise thy head, and thou shalt bruise his heel."

Covenants and Prophecies

Throughout the Old Testament, God establishes covenants and delivers prophecies that point to the ultimate restoration of creation.

- Isaiah 65:17 (KJV): "For, behold, I create new heavens and a new earth: and the former shall not be remembered, nor come into mind."

The Promise of a Messiah

The prophets foretold the coming of a Messiah who would bring about God's redemptive plan and restore creation.

- Isaiah 9:6-7 (KJV): "For unto us a child is born, unto us a son is given: and the government shall be upon his shoulder: and his name shall be called Wonderful, Counsellor, The mighty God, The everlasting Father, The Prince of Peace. Of the increase of his government and peace there shall be no end, upon the throne of David, and upon his kingdom, to order it, and to establish it with judgment and with justice from henceforth even forever. The zeal of the LORD of hosts will perform this."

The Role of Jesus in Restoration

Jesus' Ministry and the Kingdom of God

Jesus' ministry proclaimed the arrival of the Kingdom of God, demonstrating through His teachings and miracles the beginning of the restoration process.

- Luke 4:18-19 (KJV): "The Spirit of the Lord is upon me, because he hath anointed me to preach the gospel to the poor; he hath sent me to heal the brokenhearted, to preach deliverance to the captives, and recovering of sight to the blind, to set at liberty them that are bruised, To preach the acceptable year of the Lord."

The Cross and Resurrection

Jesus' death and resurrection are the pivotal events in God's plan to defeat evil and restore creation. Through His sacrifice, Jesus reconciles humanity to God and inaugurates the new creation.

- Colossians 1:19-20 (KJV): "For it pleased the Father that in him should all fulness dwell; And, having made peace through the blood of his cross, by him to reconcile all things unto himself; by him, I say, whether they be things in earth, or things in heaven."

The Promise of Jesus' Return

Jesus promised His return, at which time He will fully establish God's Kingdom, judge evil, and bring about the complete restoration of creation.

- John 14:2-3 (KJV): "In my Father's house are many mansions: if it were not so, I would have told you. I go to prepare a place for you. And if I go and prepare a place for you, I will come again, and receive you unto myself; that where I am, there ye may be also."

The Vision of a Restored Creation

The New Heaven and New Earth

The book of Revelation provides a detailed vision of the new heaven and new earth, where God dwells with His people, and all things are made new.

- Revelation 21:1-4 (KJV): "And I saw a new heaven and a new earth: for the first heaven and the first earth were passed away; and there was no more sea. And I John saw the holy city, new Jerusalem, coming down from God out of heaven, prepared as a bride adorned for her husband. And I heard a great voice out of heaven saying, Behold, the tabernacle of God is with men, and he will dwell with them, and they shall be his people, and God himself shall be with them, and be their God. And God shall wipe away all tears from their eyes; and there shall be no more death, neither sorrow, nor crying, neither shall there be any more pain: for the former things are passed away."

The Defeat of Evil

The final judgment and defeat of Satan, sin, and death are central to the vision of a restored creation. Evil is eradicated, and righteousness prevails.

- Revelation 20:10 (KJV): "And the devil that deceived them was cast into the lake of fire and brimstone, where the beast and the false prophet are, and shall be tormented day and night for ever and ever."

The Renewal of All Things

God's plan includes the renewal of all things, restoring creation to its original intended state of harmony and perfection.

- Acts 3:21 (KJV): "Whom the heaven must receive until the times of restitution of all things, which God hath spoken by the mouth of all his holy prophets since the world began."

Theological Implications of Restoration

God's Sovereignty and Faithfulness

The promise of restoration underscores God's sovereignty and faithfulness in fulfilling His promises and purposes for creation.

- Lamentations 3:22-23 (KJV): "It is of the LORD'S mercies that we are not consumed, because his compassions fail not. They are new every morning: great is thy faithfulness."

The Nature of Hope

Christian hope is rooted in the assurance of God's ultimate victory over evil and the renewal of creation. This hope sustains believers through present trials and suffering.

- Romans 8:18 (KJV): "For I reckon that the sufferings of this present time are not worthy to be compared with the glory which shall be revealed in us."

The Call to Holiness and Mission

The promise of a restored creation motivates believers to live holy lives and participate in God's redemptive mission, reflecting His kingdom values in the present world.

- 2 Peter 3:11-13 (KJV): "Seeing then that all these things shall be dissolved, what manner of persons ought ye to be in all holy conversation and godliness, Looking for and hasting unto the coming of the day of God, wherein the heavens being on fire shall be dissolved, and the elements shall melt with fervent heat? Nevertheless we, according to his promise, look for new heavens and a new earth, wherein dwelleth righteousness."

Practical Reflections on the Promise of Restoration

Living with Eternal Perspective

Believers are encouraged to live with an eternal perspective, focusing on the hope of restoration and allowing it to shape their priorities and actions.

- Colossians 3:1-2 (KJV): "If ye then be risen with Christ, seek those things which are above, where Christ sitteth on the right hand of God. Set your affection on things above, not on things on the earth."

Engaging in Creation Care

Understanding the promise of a restored creation motivates believers to care for the environment and steward God's creation responsibly.

- Genesis 2:15 (KJV): "And the LORD God took the man, and put him into the garden of Eden to dress it and to keep it."

Promoting Justice and Peace

The vision of God's Kingdom calls believers to work for justice and peace in their communities, reflecting the values of the coming restoration.

- Micah 6:8 (KJV): "He hath shewed thee, O man, what is good; and what doth the LORD require of thee, but to do justly, and to love mercy, and to walk humbly with thy God?"

Expository Study with Strong's Concordance

Restoration ("ἀποκατάστασις" apokatastasis)

The Greek word "ἀποκατάστασις" (apokatastasis), Strong's G605, means restoration or restitution. It refers to the act of restoring something to its original state or condition.

- Acts 3:21 (KJV): "Whom the heaven must receive until the times of restitution of all things, which God hath spoken by the mouth of all his holy prophets since the world began."

ew ("καινός" kainos)

The Greek word "καινός" (kainos), Strong's G2537, means new in quality or nature, as opposed to new in time. It signifies something that is fresh, unique, and superior in kind.

- Revelation 21:1 (KJV): "And I saw a new heaven and a new earth: for the first heaven and the first earth were passed away; and there was no more sea."

Comprehensive Commentary

Interpreting the Promise of Restoration

The promise of a restored creation is central to the Christian hope. It assures believers that God will ultimately defeat evil and restore all things to their intended state of harmony and perfection.

The Transformative Power of Hope

The hope of restoration transforms how believers live in the present, motivating them to pursue holiness, justice, and stewardship. It provides strength and encouragement amid suffering and trials.

Participating in God's Redemptive Work

Believers are called to participate in God's redemptive work by reflecting the values of the coming Kingdom in their daily lives. This involves acts of compassion, justice, and creation care.

The promise of a restored creation and the end of evil is a foundational aspect of Christian theology. It offers believers hope and assurance that God will fulfill His plan to defeat evil and renew all things through Jesus Christ. Understanding and embracing this promise provides a framework for living with purpose, resilience, and a commitment to God's redemptive mission. This chapter has explored the biblical foundation and practical implications of the promise of restoration, offering theological insights and reflections to help believers navigate the present world with hope and confidence in God's ultimate victory.

CHAPTER 10

LIVING IN A WORLS WITH EVIL

Practical Ways to Navigate a World with Both Good and Evil

Living in a world that contains both good and evil presents unique challenges and opportunities for believers. Navigating this complex landscape requires wisdom, faith, and practical strategies rooted in biblical principles. This chapter explores practical ways to navigate a world with both good and evil, offering guidance on how to live faithfully, uphold righteousness, and contribute positively to society.

Understanding the Reality of Good and Evil

Recognizing the Presence of Evil

Evil is a reality in the world, manifesting in various forms such as violence, injustice, suffering, and moral corruption. Acknowledging its presence is the first step in effectively navigating a world where good and evil coexist.

- 1 Peter 5:8 (KJV): "Be sober, be vigilant; because your adversary the devil, as a roaring lion, walketh about, seeking whom he may devour."

Affirming the Goodness of God

Despite the presence of evil, God remains good and sovereign. His goodness provides a foundation of hope and assurance for believers.

- Psalm 34:8 (KJV): "O taste and see that the LORD is good: blessed is the man that trusteth in him."

Cultivating Spiritual Discernment

Prayer and Meditation

Regular prayer and meditation on God's Word equip believers with spiritual discernment, enabling them to recognize and resist evil while pursuing what is good.

- Philippians 4:6-7 (KJV): "Be careful for nothing; but in every thing by prayer and supplication with thanksgiving let your requests be made known unto God. And the peace of God, which passeth all understanding, shall keep your hearts and minds through Christ Jesus."

Studying Scripture

Studying the Bible helps believers understand God's standards of good and evil, providing guidance for ethical decision-making and moral integrity.

- Psalm 119:105 (KJV): "Thy word is a lamp unto my feet, and a light unto my path."

Seeking Wise Counsel

Consulting with spiritually mature individuals can offer valuable insights and support in navigating moral complexities and making righteous choices.

- Proverbs 15:22 (KJV): "Without counsel purposes are disappointed: but in the multitude of counsellors they are established."

Living Righteously in an Evil World

Embracing Holiness

Believers are called to live holy lives, set apart for God's purposes. This involves rejecting sinful behaviors and striving to reflect God's character in all aspects of life.

- 1 Peter 1:15-16 (KJV): "But as he which hath called you is holy, so be ye holy in all manner of conversation; Because it is written, Be ye holy; for I am holy."

Practicing Love and Compassion

Demonstrating love and compassion, even toward those who do evil, reflects God's love and can be a powerful witness to the world.

- Matthew 5:44 (KJV): "But I say unto you, Love your enemies, bless them that curse you, do good to them that hate you, and pray for them which despitefully use you, and persecute you."

Engaging in Acts of Justice

Believers are called to pursue justice and defend the oppressed, working to address the root causes of evil and promote righteousness in society.

- Micah 6:8 (KJV): "He hath shewed thee, O man, what is good; and what doth the LORD require of thee, but to do justly, and to love mercy, and to walk humbly with thy God?"

Persevering in Faith

Maintaining faith in God and His promises helps believers endure hardships and remain steadfast in the face of evil.

- Hebrews 10:23 (KJV): "Let us hold fast the profession of our faith without wavering; (for he is faithful that promised;)"

Building Strong Relationships and Communities

Fostering Community

Being part of a supportive faith community provides encouragement, accountability, and resources for navigating life's challenges.

- Hebrews 10:24-25 (KJV): "And let us consider one another to provoke unto love and to good works: Not forsaking the assembling of ourselves together, as the manner of some is; but exhorting one another: and so much the more, as ye see the day approaching."

Cultivating Healthy Relationships

Healthy relationships grounded in mutual respect, love, and shared values can offer stability and support in a world filled with conflict and division.

- Ephesians 4:2-3 (KJV): "With all lowliness and meekness, with longsuffering, forbearing one another in love; Endeavouring to keep the unity of the Spirit in the bond of peace."

Mentoring and Discipleship

Mentoring and discipleship relationships can provide guidance, wisdom, and encouragement for living out one's faith in practical ways.

- 2 Timothy 2:2 (KJV): "And the things that thou hast heard of me among many witnesses, the same commit thou to faithful men, who shall be able to teach others also."

Engaging with the World

Being Salt and Light

Believers are called to influence the world positively by being salt and light, preserving what is good and illuminating the darkness.

- Matthew 5:13-16 (KJV): "Ye are the salt of the earth: but if the salt have lost his savour, wherewith shall it be salted? it is thenceforth good for nothing, but to be cast out, and to be trodden under foot of men. Ye are the light of the world. A city that is set on an hill cannot be hid. Neither do men light a candle, and put it under a bushel, but on a candlestick; and it giveth light unto all that are in the house. Let your light so shine before men, that they may see your good works, and glorify your Father which is in heaven."

Promoting Peace and Reconciliation

Actively working for peace and reconciliation helps to address conflict and build bridges between individuals and communities.

- Romans 12:18 (KJV): "If it be possible, as much as lieth in you, live peaceably with all men."

Advocating for Truth and Justice

Standing up for truth and justice involves challenging falsehoods, advocating for the marginalized, and working to rectify injustices.

- Proverbs 31:8-9 (KJV): "Open thy mouth for the dumb in the cause of all such as are appointed to destruction. Open thy mouth, judge righteously, and plead the cause of the poor and needy."

Personal Spiritual Practices

Daily Devotion and Worship

Regular devotion and worship strengthen one's relationship with God, providing spiritual nourishment and resilience against evil.

- Psalm 63:1 (KJV): "O God, thou art my God; early will I seek thee: my soul thirsteth for thee, my flesh longeth for thee in a dry and thirsty land, where no water is."

Confession and Repentance

Practicing confession and repentance helps maintain a clear conscience and a right relationship with God.

- 1 John 1:9 (KJV): "If we confess our sins, he is faithful and just to forgive us our sins, and to cleanse us from all unrighteousness."

Cultivating Gratitude

Maintaining an attitude of gratitude shifts focus from the negative aspects of life to God's blessings, fostering joy and contentment.

- 1 Thessalonians 5:18 (KJV): "In every thing give thanks: for this is the will of God in Christ Jesus concerning you."

Practical Steps for Daily Living

Setting Boundaries

Setting personal boundaries helps protect against negative influences and maintain spiritual health.

- Proverbs 4:23 (KJV): "Keep thy heart with all diligence; for out of it are the issues of life."

Managing Time Wisely

Wisely managing time and priorities ensures that one's life aligns with God's purposes and values.

- Ephesians 5:15-16 (KJV): "See then that ye walk circumspectly, not as fools, but as wise, Redeeming the time, because the days are evil."

Engaging in Self-Care

Taking care of one's physical, emotional, and mental health enables individuals to serve God and others effectively.

- 1 Corinthians 6:19-20 (KJV): "What? know ye not that your body is the temple of the Holy Ghost which is in you, which ye have of God, and ye are not your own? For ye are bought with a price: therefore glorify God in your body, and in your spirit, which are God's."

Expository Study with Strong's Concordance

Good ("ἀγαθός" agathos)

The Greek word "ἀγαθός" (agathos), Strong's G18, means good, beneficial, or virtuous. It signifies what is morally right and pleasing to God.

- Romans 12:21 (KJV): "Be not overcome of evil, but overcome evil with good."

Evil ("πονηρός" ponēros)

The Greek word "πονηρός" (ponēros), Strong's G4190, means evil, wicked, or malicious. It encompasses moral evil and the malevolent actions of individuals and spiritual forces.

- Matthew 6:13 (KJV): "And lead us not into temptation, but deliver us from evil: For thine is the kingdom, and the power, and the glory, for ever. Amen."

Comprehensive Commentary

Balancing Good and Evil in Daily Life

Navigating a world with both good and evil requires a balanced approach that recognizes the reality of evil while actively pursuing good. Believers are called to be vigilant, discerning, and proactive in their efforts to uphold righteousness and resist evil.

The Role of Community and Relationships

Healthy relationships and supportive faith communities provide the necessary foundation for navigating moral complexities. These networks offer encouragement, accountability, and shared wisdom, helping individuals to live out their faith effectively.

Practical Application of Spiritual Principles

Implementing spiritual principles in daily life involves regular devotion, ethical decision-making, and active engagement with the world. Believers are called to be salt and light, promoting justice, peace, and reconciliation in their spheres of influence.

Living in a world with both good and evil presents significant challenges, but also opportunities for believers to reflect God's character and advance His kingdom. By cultivating spiritual discernment, embracing holiness, engaging with the world, and fostering strong relationships, believers can navigate this complex landscape effectively. This chapter has provided practical ways to live faithfully in a world with both good and evil, offering guidance and encouragement rooted in biblical principles.

The Christian Call to Goodness and Holiness

The call to goodness and holiness is central to the Christian faith. It encompasses both moral integrity and spiritual purity, reflecting the character of God in every aspect of life. This chapter explores the biblical foundation for this call, the practical ways to live it out, and the transformative impact it has on individuals and communities.

The Biblical Foundation for Goodness and Holiness

God's Character as the Standard

God's nature is the ultimate standard for goodness and holiness. Believers are called to emulate His character in their lives.

- Leviticus 11:44 (KJV): "For I am the LORD your God: ye shall therefore sanctify yourselves, and ye shall be holy; for I am holy."

- 1 John 1:5 (KJV): "This then is the message which we have heard of him, and declare unto you, that God is light, and in him is no darkness at all."

Jesus as the Model of Holiness

Jesus Christ exemplifies perfect goodness and holiness. His life provides the model for how believers are to live.

- 1 Peter 2:21-22 (KJV): "For even hereunto were ye called: because Christ also suffered for us, leaving us an example, that ye should follow his steps: Who did no sin, neither was guile found in his mouth."

The Work of the Holy Spirit

The Holy Spirit empowers believers to live lives of goodness and holiness, transforming their character and enabling them to bear fruit.

- Galatians 5:22-23 (KJV): "But the fruit of the Spirit is love, joy, peace, longsuffering, gentleness, goodness, faith, Meekness, temperance: against such there is no law."

- 1 Corinthians 6:11 (KJV): "And such were some of you: but ye are washed, but ye are sanctified, but ye are justified in the name of the Lord Jesus, and by the Spirit of our God."

The Call to Goodness

Defining Goodness

Goodness involves moral excellence, kindness, and a commitment to doing what is right. It reflects God's goodness and is manifested in ethical behavior and acts of compassion.

- Micah 6:8 (KJV): "He hath shewed thee, O man, what is good; and what doth the LORD require of thee, but to do justly, and to love mercy, and to walk humbly with thy God?"

Living Out Goodness in Daily Life

Believers are called to practice goodness in all areas of life, including relationships, work, and community involvement.

- Romans 12:9-10 (KJV): "Let love be without dissimulation. Abhor that which is evil; cleave to that which is good. Be kindly affectioned one to another with brotherly love; in honour preferring one another."

The Role of Good Works

Good works are a natural outflow of a transformed heart. They do not earn salvation but are a response to God's grace and a testimony to others.

- Ephesians 2:10 (KJV): "For we are his workmanship, created in Christ Jesus unto good works, which God hath before ordained that we should walk in them."

The Call to Holiness

Defining Holiness

Holiness means being set apart for God's purposes, living in purity, and avoiding sin. It involves both moral integrity and spiritual consecration.

- 1 Peter 1:15-16 (KJV): "But as he which hath called you is holy, so be ye holy in all manner of conversation; Because it is written, Be ye holy; for I am holy."

Sanctification Process

Sanctification is the ongoing process of becoming more like Christ. It involves daily commitment, spiritual disciplines, and reliance on the Holy Spirit.

- Philippians 2:12-13 (KJV): "Wherefore, my beloved, as ye have always obeyed, not as in my presence only, but now much more in my absence, work out your own salvation with fear and trembling. For it is God which worketh in you both to will and to do of his good pleasure."

Holiness in Thought and Action

Holiness encompasses both inward purity and outward conduct. Believers are called to guard their hearts and minds and to live out their faith in tangible ways.

- Philippians 4:8 (KJV): "Finally, brethren, whatsoever things are true, whatsoever things are honest, whatsoever things are just, whatsoever things are pure, whatsoever things are lovely, whatsoever things are of good report; if there be any virtue, and if there be any praise, think on these things."

- James 1:27 (KJV): "Pure religion and undefiled before God and the Father is this, To visit the fatherless and widows in their affliction, and to keep himself unspotted from the world."

Practical Ways to Cultivate Goodness and Holiness

Prayer and Devotion

Regular prayer and devotion help believers stay connected to God, seek His guidance, and align their lives with His will.

- 1 Thessalonians 5:17 (KJV): "Pray without ceasing."

Studying Scripture

Studying the Bible provides the foundation for understanding God's standards and growing in knowledge and wisdom.

- 2 Timothy 3:16-17 (KJV): "All scripture is given by inspiration of God, and is profitable for doctrine, for reproof, for correction, for instruction in righteousness: That the man of God may be perfect, throughly furnished unto all good works."

Fellowship and Accountability

Being part of a faith community offers support, encouragement, and accountability, helping believers stay committed to goodness and holiness.

- Hebrews 10:24-25 (KJV): "And let us consider one another to provoke unto love and to good works: Not forsaking the assembling of ourselves together, as the manner of some is; but exhorting one another: and so much the more, as ye see the day approaching."

Serving Others

Serving others reflects God's love and goodness, fostering a spirit of humility and compassion.

- Galatians 5:13 (KJV): "For, brethren, ye have been called unto liberty; only use not liberty for an occasion to the flesh, but by love serve one another."

Avoiding Temptation

Believers are called to avoid situations and influences that lead to sin, seeking to live pure and blameless lives.

- 1 Corinthians 10:13 (KJV): "There hath no temptation taken you but such as is common to man: but God is faithful, who will not suffer you to be tempted above that ye are able; but will with the temptation also make a way to escape, that ye may be able to bear it."

The Impact of Goodness and Holiness

Personal Transformation

Living in goodness and holiness transforms individuals, helping them to grow in Christlikeness and experience the fullness of life in Christ.

- 2 Corinthians 5:17 (KJV): "Therefore if any man be in Christ, he is a new creature: old things are passed away; behold, all things are become new."

Witness to the World

Goodness and holiness serve as a powerful witness to the world, drawing others to Christ and demonstrating the reality of God's kingdom.

- Matthew 5:16 (KJV): "Let your light so shine before men, that they may see your good works, and glorify your Father which is in heaven."

Strengthening the Church

A commitment to goodness and holiness strengthens the church, fostering unity, love, and effective ministry.

- Ephesians 4:1-3 (KJV): "I therefore, the prisoner of the Lord, beseech you that ye walk worthy of the vocation wherewith ye are called, With all lowliness and meekness, with longsuffering, forbearing one another in love; Endeavouring to keep the unity of the Spirit in the bond of peace."

Expository Study with Strong's Concordance

Goodness ("ἀγαθωσύνη" agathōsynē)

The Greek word "ἀγαθωσύνη" (agathōsynē), Strong's G19, means goodness, virtue, or beneficence. It signifies moral excellence and active kindness.

- Galatians 5:22 (KJV): "But the fruit of the Spirit is love, joy, peace, longsuffering, gentleness, goodness, faith."

Holiness ("ἀγιότης" hagiotēs)

The Greek word "ἀγιότης" (hagiotēs), Strong's G42, means holiness or sanctity. It refers to being set apart for God and living in moral purity.

- Hebrews 12:10 (KJV): "For they verily for a few days chastened us after their own pleasure; but he for our profit, that we might be partakers of his holiness."

Comprehensive Commentary

Understanding the Call to Goodness and Holiness

The call to goodness and holiness is an invitation to reflect God's character and participate in His redemptive work in the world. It involves a commitment to moral integrity, spiritual purity, and active compassion.

Living Out the Call in Practical Ways

Practical ways to cultivate goodness and holiness include regular prayer and devotion, studying Scripture, participating in fellowship, serving others, and avoiding temptation. These practices help believers grow in their relationship with God and live out their faith authentically

The Transformative Impact of Goodness and Holiness

Living in goodness and holiness transforms individuals, strengthens the church, and serves as a powerful witness to the world. It reflects the reality of God's kingdom and draws others to Christ.

The Christian call to goodness and holiness is foundational to the faith. It reflects God's character and transforms individuals and communities. By embracing this call and living it out in practical ways, believers can experience the fullness of life in Christ and contribute to His redemptive work in the world. This chapter has explored the biblical foundation, practical application, and transformative impact of goodness and holiness, offering guidance and encouragement for believers committed to this call.

Examples of How Faith Can Overcome Evil

Faith is a powerful force that enables believers to overcome evil and navigate the challenges of a fallen world. Throughout history and Scripture, there are numerous examples of how faith has triumphed over evil, demonstrating God's power and faithfulness. This chapter explores biblical and contemporary examples of how faith can overcome evil, offering inspiration and practical insights for believers today.

Biblical Examples of Faith Overcoming Evil

David and Goliath

David's faith in God allowed him to defeat Goliath, a giant Philistine warrior who threatened Israel. Despite his youth and inexperience, David's trust in God enabled him to achieve a miraculous victory.

- 1 Samuel 17:45-47 (KJV): "Then said David to the Philistine, Thou comest to me with a sword, and with a spear, and with a shield: but I come to thee in the name of the LORD of hosts, the God of the armies of Israel, whom thou hast defied. This day will the LORD deliver thee into mine hand; and I will smite thee, and take thine head from thee; and I will give the carcases of the host of the Philistines this day unto the fowls of the air, and to the wild beasts of the earth;

that all the earth may know that there is a God in Israel. And all this assembly shall know that the LORD saveth not with sword and spear: for the battle is the LORD'S, and he will give you into our hands."

Daniel in the Lion's Den

Daniel's unwavering faith led to his miraculous deliverance from the lion's den. Despite facing persecution for his devotion to God, Daniel remained steadfast, and God protected him.

- Daniel 6:22-23 (KJV): "My God hath sent his angel, and hath shut the lions' mouths, that they have not hurt me: forasmuch as before him innocency was found in me; and also before thee, O king, have I done no hurt. Then was the king exceeding glad for him, and commanded that they should take Daniel up out of the den. So Daniel was taken up out of the den, and no manner of hurt was found upon him, because he believed in his God."

Esther's Courage

Queen Esther's faith and courage saved the Jewish people from annihilation. By risking her life to approach the king, Esther exposed the evil plot against her people and secured their deliverance.

- Esther 4:16 (KJV): "Go, gather together all the Jews that are present in Shushan, and fast ye for me, and neither eat nor drink three days, night or day: I also and my maidens will fast likewise; and so will I go in unto the king, which is not according to the law: and if I perish, I perish."

The Apostles' Boldness

The apostles' faith empowered them to preach the gospel boldly, despite facing severe persecution. Their unwavering commitment to Christ and reliance on the Holy Spirit enabled them to overcome evil and spread the message of salvation.

- Acts 4:29-31 (KJV): "And now, Lord, behold their threatenings: and grant unto thy servants, that with all boldness they may speak thy word, By stretching forth thine hand to heal; and that signs and wonders may be done by the name of thy holy child Jesus. And when they had prayed, the place was shaken where they were assembled together; and they were all filled with the Holy Ghost, and they spake the word of God with boldness."

Paul's Perseverance

The Apostle Paul faced numerous trials, including imprisonment, beatings, and shipwrecks. His faith and perseverance in the face of these evils allowed him to spread the gospel and strengthen the early church.

- 2 Corinthians 11:24-28 (KJV): "Of the Jews five times received I forty stripes save one. Thrice was I beaten with rods, once was I stoned, thrice I suffered shipwreck, a night and a day I have been in the deep; In journeyings often, in perils of waters, in perils of robbers, in perils by mine own countrymen, in perils by the heathen, in perils in the city, in perils in the wilderness, in perils in the sea, in perils among false brethren; In weariness and painfulness, in watchings often, in hunger and thirst, in fastings often, in cold and nakedness. Beside those things that are without, that which cometh upon me daily, the care of all the churches."

Contemporary Examples of Faith Overcoming Evil

Corrie ten Boom

During World War II, Corrie ten Boom and her family hid Jews from the Nazis, driven by their Christian faith. Despite being arrested and sent to a concentration camp, Corrie's faith helped her endure unimaginable suffering. After the war, she preached forgiveness and reconciliation, demonstrating the power of faith to overcome hatred and evil.

- Corrie ten Boom's Quote: "There is no pit so deep, that God's love is not deeper still."

Martin Luther King Jr.

Dr. Martin Luther King Jr.'s faith inspired his leadership in the Civil Rights Movement. His commitment to nonviolent resistance and his belief in the power of love and justice helped dismantle systemic racism and bring about significant social change.

- Martin Luther King Jr.'s Quote: "Darkness cannot drive out darkness; only light can do that. Hate cannot drive out hate; only love can do that."

Dietrich Bonhoeffer

Dietrich Bonhoeffer, a German pastor and theologian, stood against the evil of the Nazi regime. His faith led him to participate in resistance efforts and ultimately cost him his life. His writings continue to inspire Christians to stand firm in their convictions.

- Dietrich Bonhoeffer's Quote: "When Christ calls a man, he bids him come and die."

Mother Teresa

Mother Teresa's faith drove her to serve the poorest of the poor in Calcutta, India. Her life of selfless love and compassion overcame the evils of poverty and neglect, bringing hope and dignity to countless individuals.

- Mother Teresa's Quote: "Faith in action is love, and love in action is service."

Theological Insights on Faith and Overcoming Evil
The Nature of Faith

Faith is trust in God's character and promises, even in the face of evil. It involves believing in God's sovereignty, goodness, and ultimate victory over evil.

- Hebrews 11:1 (KJV): "Now faith is the substance of things hoped for, the evidence of things not seen."

The Power of Prayer

Prayer is a vital expression of faith that aligns believers with God's will and releases His power to overcome evil.

- James 5:16 (KJV): "The effectual fervent prayer of a righteous man availeth much."

The Role of the Holy Spirit

The Holy Spirit empowers believers to stand firm against evil, providing guidance, strength, and comfort.

- Ephesians 3:16 (KJV): "That he would grant you, according to the riches of his glory, to be strengthened with might by his Spirit in the inner man."

The Victory of Christ

Jesus' life, death, and resurrection provide the ultimate victory over evil. Believers participate in this victory through faith, living out the implications of Christ's triumph.

- 1 Corinthians 15:57 (KJV): "But thanks be to God, which giveth us the victory through our Lord Jesus Christ."

Practical Applications of Faith in Overcoming Evil

Standing Firm in Faith

Believers are called to stand firm in their faith, trusting God's promises and resisting the temptation to compromise with evil.

- Ephesians 6:13 (KJV): "Wherefore take unto you the whole armour of God, that ye may be able to withstand in the evil day, and having done all, to stand."

Practicing Forgiveness

Forgiveness is a powerful act of faith that breaks the cycle of evil and reflects God's grace.

- Matthew 6:14-15 (KJV): "For if ye forgive men their trespasses, your heavenly Father will also forgive you: But if ye forgive not men their trespasses, neither will your Father forgive your trespasses."

Engaging in Acts of Love and Justice

Faith motivates believers to engage in acts of love and justice, confronting evil and promoting the values of God's kingdom.

- Micah 6:8 (KJV): "He hath shewed thee, O man, what is good; and what doth the LORD require of thee, but to do justly, and to love mercy, and to walk humbly with thy God?"

Cultivating a Life of Prayer and Worship

Regular prayer and worship strengthen faith and keep believers focused on God's presence and power.

- Philippians 4:6-7 (KJV): "Be careful for nothing; but in every thing by prayer and supplication with thanksgiving let your requests be made known unto God. And the peace of God, which passeth all understanding, shall keep your hearts and minds through Christ Jesus."

Building a Supportive Community

Being part of a faith community provides encouragement, accountability, and resources for overcoming evil.

- Hebrews 10:24-25 (KJV): "And let us consider one another to provoke unto love and to good works: Not forsaking the assembling of ourselves together, as the manner of some is; but exhorting one another: and so much the more, as ye see the day approaching."

Expository Study with Strong's Concordance

Faith ("πίστις" pistis)

The Greek word "πίστις" (pistis), Strong's G4102, means faith, belief, or trust. It signifies a firm conviction and reliance upon God.

- Hebrews 11:6 (KJV): "But without faith it is impossible to please him: for he that cometh to God must believe that he is, and that he is a rewarder of them that diligently seek him."

Overcome ("νικάω" nikaō)

The Greek word "νικάω" (nikaō), Strong's G3528, means to conquer, overcome, or prevail. It emphasizes victory over obstacles and adversaries.

- 1 John 5:4 (KJV): "For whatsoever is born of God overcometh the world: and this is the victory that overcometh the world, even our faith."

Comprehensive Commentary

The Power of Faith in Action

Faith in action has the power to overcome evil and bring about transformative change. This power is evident in both biblical and contemporary examples, where individuals and communities have relied on God's strength to confront and conquer evil.

Living Out Faith in Daily Life

Living out faith involves standing firm in trust, practicing forgiveness, engaging in love and justice, cultivating prayer and worship, and building supportive communities. These practices help believers navigate a world filled with evil and reflect God's kingdom on earth.

The Ultimate Victory in Christ

The ultimate victory over evil is found in Jesus Christ. Believers participate in this victory through faith, experiencing God's power and presence in their lives and witnessing to the world.

Faith is a powerful and transformative force that enables believers to overcome evil and reflect God's goodness in the world. By examining biblical and contemporary examples, understanding theological insights, and applying practical strategies, believers can navigate the challenges of a fallen world with confidence and hope. This chapter has explored how faith can overcome evil, offering inspiration and guidance for living a victorious Christian life.

CHAPTER 11

THE FUTURE HOPE

Eschatological Views on the End of Evil

Eschatology, the study of the last things, provides Christians with a hopeful perspective on the future and the ultimate end of evil. The Bible presents a clear vision of God's plan to defeat evil, restore creation, and establish His eternal kingdom. This chapter explores various eschatological views on the end of evil, examining key biblical passages, theological interpretations, and the practical implications of these beliefs for believers today.

Biblical Foundation for Eschatology

The Prophetic Hope in the Old Testament

The Old Testament contains numerous prophecies about the end times, emphasizing the defeat of evil and the establishment of God's kingdom.

- Isaiah 2:4 (KJV): "And he shall judge among the nations, and shall rebuke many people: and they shall beat their swords into plowshares, and their spears into pruninghooks: nation shall not lift up sword against nation, neither shall they learn war any more."

- Daniel 7:14 (KJV): "And there was given him dominion, and glory, and a kingdom, that all people, nations, and languages, should serve him: his dominion is an everlasting dominion, which shall not pass away, and his kingdom that which shall not be destroyed."

Jesus' Teachings on the End Times

Jesus spoke extensively about the end times, highlighting the coming judgment, the resurrection of the dead, and the final victory over evil.

- Matthew 24:30-31 (KJV): "And then shall appear the sign of the Son of man in heaven: and then shall all the tribes of the earth mourn, and they shall see the Son of man coming in the clouds of heaven with power and great glory. And he shall send his angels with a great sound of a trumpet, and they shall gather together his elect from the four winds, from one end of heaven to the other."

The Book of Revelation

The Book of Revelation provides a detailed and symbolic portrayal of the end times, including the final defeat of Satan, the judgment of the wicked, and the establishment of a new heaven and a new earth.

- Revelation 20:10 (KJV): "And the devil that deceived them was cast into the lake of fire and brimstone, where the beast and the false prophet are, and shall be tormented day and night for ever and ever."

- Revelation 21:1-4 (KJV): "And I saw a new heaven and a new earth: for the first heaven and the first earth were passed away; and there was no more sea. And I John saw the holy city, new Jerusalem, coming down from God out of heaven, prepared as a bride adorned for her husband. And I heard a great voice out of heaven saying, Behold, the tabernacle of God is with men, and he will dwell with them, and they shall be his people, and God himself shall be with them, and be their God. And God shall wipe away all tears from their eyes; and there shall be no more death, neither sorrow, nor crying, neither shall there be any more pain: for the former things are passed away."

Key Eschatological Views

Premillennialism

Premillennialism teaches that Jesus will return before a literal thousand-year reign (the Millennium). This view emphasizes a period of tribulation followed by Christ's second coming, the binding of Satan, and a literal reign of peace and righteousness.

- Revelation 20:1-6 (KJV): "And I saw an angel come down from heaven, having the key of the bottomless pit and a great chain in his hand. And he laid hold on the dragon, that old serpent, which is the Devil, and Satan, and bound him a thousand years, And cast him into the bottomless pit, and shut him up, and set a seal upon him, that he should deceive the nations no more, till the thousand years should be fulfilled: and after that he must be loosed a little season. And I saw thrones, and they sat upon them, and judgment was given unto them: and I saw the souls of them that were beheaded for the witness of Jesus, and for the word of God, and which had not worshipped the beast, neither his image, neither had received his mark upon their foreheads, or in their hands; and they lived and reigned with Christ a thousand years. But the rest of the dead lived not again until the thousand years were finished. This is the first resurrection. Blessed and holy is he that hath part in the first resurrection: on such the second death hath no power, but they shall be priests of God and of Christ, and shall reign with him a thousand years."

Amillennialism

Amillennialism interprets the Millennium symbolically rather than literally, viewing it as the current reign of Christ through His Church. This view holds that the binding of Satan occurred at Christ's first coming and that the end times culminate in the final judgment and the new creation.

- Colossians 1:13 (KJV): "Who hath delivered us from the power of darkness, and hath translated us into the kingdom of his dear Son."

- John 5:28-29 (KJV): "Marvel not at this: for the hour is coming, in the which all that are in the graves shall hear his voice, And shall come forth; they that have done good, unto the resurrection of life; and they that have done evil, unto the resurrection of damnation."

Postmillennialism

Postmillennialism teaches that Christ will return after a period of widespread peace and righteousness, often referred to as the Millennium. This view emphasizes the transformative power of the gospel to bring about significant positive change in the world before Christ's second coming.

- Matthew 13:33 (KJV): "Another parable spake he unto them; The kingdom of heaven is like unto leaven, which a woman took, and hid in three measures of meal, till the whole was leavened."

- Isaiah 11:9 (KJV): "They shall not hurt nor destroy in all my holy mountain: for the earth shall be full of the knowledge of the LORD, as the waters cover the sea."

Preterism

Preterism interprets many of the eschatological prophecies as having already been fulfilled, particularly those in the Book of Revelation. Full Preterists believe all prophecy was fulfilled by AD 70 with the destruction of Jerusalem, while Partial Preterists believe that some prophecies are still future.

- Matthew 24:34 (KJV): "Verily I say unto you, This generation shall not pass, till all these things be fulfilled."

The Defeat of Evil in Eschatological Perspective

The Final Judgment

The Bible teaches that there will be a final judgment where God will hold every person accountable for their actions. This judgment will result in the ultimate defeat of evil and the vindication of the righteous.

- Revelation 20:11-15 (KJV): "And I saw a great white throne, and him that sat on it, from whose face the earth and the heaven fled away; and there was found no place for them. And I saw the dead, small and great, stand before God; and the books were opened: and another book was opened, which is the book of life: and the dead were judged out of those things which were written in the books, according to their works. And the sea gave up the dead which were in it; and death and hell delivered up the dead which were in them: and they were judged every man according to their works. And death and hell were cast into the lake of fire. This is the second death. And whosoever was not found written in the book of life was cast into the lake of fire."

The Binding and Defeat of Satan

Satan, the ultimate source of evil, will be bound and ultimately defeated, preventing him from deceiving the nations and bringing about his eternal punishment.

- Revelation 20:1-3 (KJV): "And I saw an angel come down from heaven, having the key of the bottomless pit and a great chain in his hand. And he laid hold on the dragon, that old serpent, which is the Devil, and Satan, and bound him a thousand years, And cast him into the bottomless pit, and shut him up, and set a seal upon him, that he should deceive the nations no more, till the thousand years should be fulfilled: and after that he must be loosed a little season."

The New Heaven and New Earth

The ultimate promise of eschatology is the creation of a new heaven and a new earth where evil, suffering, and death are no more. This renewed creation will be characterized by God's presence, peace, and eternal joy.

- Revelation 21:1-4 (KJV): "And I saw a new heaven and a new earth: for the first heaven and the first earth were passed away; and there was no more sea. And I John saw the holy city, new Jerusalem, coming down from God out of heaven, prepared as a bride adorned for her husband. And I heard a great voice out of heaven saying, Behold, the tabernacle of God is with men, and he will dwell with them, and they shall be his people, and God himself shall be with them, and be their God. And God shall wipe away all tears from their eyes; and there shall be no more death, neither sorrow, nor crying, neither shall there be any more pain: for the former things are passed away."

Practical Implications of Eschatological Beliefs

Living with Hope

Eschatological beliefs provide believers with hope and assurance that evil will ultimately be defeated and that God's kingdom will be fully realized.

- 1 Thessalonians 4:16-18 (KJV): "For the Lord himself shall descend from heaven with a shout, with the voice of the archangel, and with the trump of God: and the dead in Christ shall rise first: Then we which are alive and remain shall be caught up together with them in the clouds, to meet the Lord in the air: and so shall we ever be with the Lord. Wherefore comfort one another with these words."

Motivation for Holy Living

The anticipation of Christ's return and the final judgment motivates believers to live holy and righteous lives, reflecting the values of God's kingdom.

- 2 Peter 3:11-12 (KJV): "Seeing then that all these things shall be dissolved, what manner of persons ought ye to be in all holy conversation and godliness, Looking for and hasting unto the coming of the day of God, wherein the heavens being on fire shall be dissolved, and the elements shall melt with fervent heat?"

Engaging in Mission and Evangelism

The belief in the imminent return of Christ and the final defeat of evil drives believers to share the gospel and engage in mission, seeking to bring others into the knowledge of God's saving grace.

- Matthew 28:19-20 (KJV): "Go ye therefore, and teach all nations, baptizing them in the name of the Father, and of the Son, and of the Holy Ghost: Teaching them to observe all things whatsoever I have commanded you: and, lo, I am with you alway, even unto the end of the world. Amen."

Promoting Justice and Peace

Understanding God's ultimate plan for justice and peace encourages believers to work toward these goals in the present world, striving to reflect God's kingdom here and now.

- Isaiah 58:6-7 (KJV): "Is not this the fast that I have chosen? to loose the bands of wickedness, to undo the heavy burdens, and to let the oppressed go free, and that ye break every yoke? Is it not to deal thy bread to the hungry, and that thou bring the poor that are cast out to thy house? when thou seest the naked, that thou cover him; and that thou hide not thyself from thine own flesh?"

Expository Study with Strong's Concordance

Eschatology ("ἔσχατος" eschatos)

The Greek word "ἔσχατος" (eschatos), Strong's G2078, means last or final. It refers to the study of the last things, including the end times, the return of Christ, and the final judgment.

- 1 Peter 1:5 (KJV): "Who are kept by the power of God through faith unto salvation ready to be revealed in the last time."

Hope ("ἐλπίς" elpis)

The Greek word "ἐλπίς" (elpis), Strong's G1680, means hope or expectation. It signifies the confident expectation of God's promises being fulfilled.

- Romans 8:24-25 (KJV): "For we are saved by hope: but hope that is seen is not hope: for what a man seeth, why doth he yet hope for? But if we hope for that we see not, then do we with patience wait for it."

Comprehensive Commentary

Understanding Eschatological Views

Eschatology provides a framework for understanding God's ultimate plan for the defeat of evil and the restoration of creation. Different eschatological views offer various interpretations of how these events will unfold, but all emphasize God's sovereignty and the final victory of good over evil.

Living in Light of Eschatological Hope

Believers are called to live in light of the hope provided by eschatology. This involves living holy lives, engaging in mission and evangelism, promoting justice and peace, and maintaining a confident expectation of God's promises.

The Transformative Power of Eschatology

The study of eschatology has a transformative impact on believers, shaping their worldview, priorities, and actions.

It encourages perseverance, inspires hope, and motivates a life dedicated to reflecting God's kingdom on earth.

Eschatology offers a hopeful perspective on the future and the ultimate end of evil. By exploring various eschatological views, understanding their biblical foundations, and considering their practical implications, believers can navigate the present world with confidence and purpose. This chapter has examined eschatological views on the end of evil, providing theological insights and practical guidance for living in light of God's ultimate victory.

The Promise of a New Heaven and New Earth

The promise of a new heaven and new earth is a central theme in Christian eschatology, offering believers hope and assurance of God's ultimate plan for the restoration of all things. This chapter explores the biblical foundations of this promise, its theological significance, and the practical implications for believers today. Understanding this promise provides a profound sense of purpose and anticipation for the future, as well as guidance for living faithfully in the present.

Biblical Foundations of the New Heaven and New Earth

Old Testament Prophecies

The concept of a renewed creation is rooted in Old Testament prophecies that envision a future where God's justice and peace reign supreme.

- Isaiah 65:17 (KJV): "For, behold, I create new heavens and a new earth: and the former shall not be remembered, nor come into mind."

- Isaiah 66:22 (KJV): "For as the new heavens and the new earth, which I will make, shall remain before me, saith the LORD, so shall your seed and your name remain."

New Testament Fulfillment

The New Testament further develops this promise, emphasizing the transformation and renewal that will occur through Christ's return.

- 2 Peter 3:13 (KJV): "Nevertheless we, according to his promise, look for new heavens and a new earth, wherein dwelleth righteousness."

- Revelation 21:1-4 (KJV): "And I saw a new heaven and a new earth: for the first heaven and the first earth were passed away; and there was no more sea. And I John saw the holy city, new Jerusalem, coming down from God out of heaven, prepared as a bride adorned for her husband. And I heard a great voice out of heaven saying, Behold, the tabernacle of God is with men, and he will dwell with them, and they shall be his people, and God himself shall be with them, and be their God. And God shall wipe away all tears from their eyes; and there shall be no more death, neither sorrow, nor crying, neither shall there be any more pain: for the former things are passed away."

Theological Significance of the New Heaven and New Earth

The Fulfillment of God's Redemptive Plan

The creation of a new heaven and new earth represents the culmination of God's redemptive plan, where all things are restored to their intended glory.

- Ephesians 1:10 (KJV): "That in the dispensation of the fulness of times he might gather together in one all things in Christ, both which are in heaven, and which are on earth; even in him."

The Defeat of Evil and Sin

In the new creation, evil and sin are completely eradicated, and God's righteousness and holiness prevail.

- Revelation 21:27 (KJV): "And there shall in no wise enter into it any thing that defileth, neither whatsoever worketh abomination, or maketh a lie: but they which are written in the Lamb's book of life."

Eternal Communion with God

The promise of a new heaven and new earth emphasizes eternal communion with God, where His presence is fully manifest among His people.

- Revelation 22:3-4 (KJV): "And there shall be no more curse: but the throne of God and of the Lamb shall be in it; and his servants shall serve him: And they shall see his face; and his name shall be in their foreheads."

Characteristics of the New Heaven and New Earth

A Place of Perfect Peace and Justice

The new creation will be characterized by perfect peace and justice, where God's will is done perfectly.

- Isaiah 11:6-9 (KJV): "The wolf also shall dwell with the lamb, and the leopard shall lie down with the kid; and the calf and the young lion and the fatling together; and a little child shall lead them. And the cow and the bear shall feed; their young ones shall lie down together: and the lion shall eat straw like the ox. And the sucking child shall play on the hole of the asp, and the weaned child shall put his hand on the cockatrice' den. They shall not hurt nor destroy in all my holy mountain: for the earth shall be full of the knowledge of the LORD, as the waters cover the sea."

A Place of Beauty and Abundance

The new heaven and new earth will reflect the beauty and abundance of God's original creation, unmarred by sin and decay.

- Revelation 22:1-2 (KJV): "And he shewed me a pure river of water of life, clear as crystal, proceeding out of the throne of God and of the Lamb. In the midst of the street of it, and on either side of the river, was there the tree of life, which bare twelve manner of fruits, and yielded her fruit every month: and the leaves of the tree were for the healing of the nations."

A Place of Eternal Life and Joy

Eternal life and joy are hallmarks of the new creation, where death and suffering are no more.

- Revelation 21:4 (KJV): "And God shall wipe away all tears from their eyes; and there shall be no more death, neither sorrow, nor crying, neither shall there be any more pain: for the former things are passed away."

Practical Implications for Believers

Living with Hope and Expectation

The promise of a new heaven and new earth provides believers with hope and a future-oriented perspective, encouraging them to live in light of God's ultimate plan.

- Romans 8:18 (KJV): "For I reckon that the sufferings of this present time are not worthy to be compared with the glory which shall be revealed in us."

Pursuing Holiness and Righteousness

Knowing that God's new creation will be characterized by holiness and righteousness motivates believers to pursue these qualities in their lives.

- 2 Peter 3:11 (KJV): "Seeing then that all these things shall be dissolved, what manner of persons ought ye to be in all holy conversation and godliness."

Engaging in Creation Care

The promise of a restored creation encourages believers to care for the environment and steward God's creation responsibly.

- Genesis 2:15 (KJV): "And the LORD God took the man, and put him into the garden of Eden to dress it and to keep it."

Working for Justice and Peace

Believers are called to work for justice and peace in anticipation of the new creation, reflecting God's kingdom values in the present world.

- Micah 6:8 (KJV): "He hath shewed thee, O man, what is good; and what doth the LORD require of thee, but to do justly, and to love mercy, and to walk humbly with thy God?"

Expository Study with Strong's Concordance

New ("καινός" kainos)

The Greek word "καινός" (kainos), Strong's G2537, means new in quality or nature, as opposed to new in time. It signifies something that is fresh, unique, and superior in kind.

- Revelation 21:1 (KJV): "And I saw a new heaven and a new earth: for the first heaven and the first earth were passed away; and there was no more sea."

Heaven ("οὐρανός" ouranos)

The Greek word "οὐρανός" (ouranos), Strong's G3772, refers to the sky, the celestial realm, or the abode of God. In eschatological contexts, it signifies the renewed realm where God dwells with His people.

- Matthew 5:12 (KJV): "Rejoice, and be exceeding glad: for great is your reward in heaven: for so persecuted they the prophets which were before you."

Comprehensive Commentary

Theological Significance of the New Creation

The promise of a new heaven and new earth is foundational to Christian eschatology, symbolizing the fulfillment of God's redemptive plan and the ultimate triumph of good over evil. It underscores God's commitment to restore His creation to its intended glory and to dwell eternally with His people.

Living in Light of the New Creation

Believers are called to live in anticipation of the new creation, allowing this future hope to shape their present actions and attitudes. This involves pursuing holiness, engaging in acts of justice and mercy, caring for the environment, and sharing the gospel.

The Transformative Power of Eschatological Hope

The hope of a new heaven and new earth transforms how believers view their lives and the world around them. It provides a sense of purpose, resilience in the face of suffering, and motivation to live according to God's kingdom values.

The promise of a new heaven and new earth is a cornerstone of Christian eschatology, offering believers a vision of a restored creation where God dwells with His people in perfect peace, justice, and joy. By understanding this promise and its theological significance, believers can live with hope and purpose, anticipating the fulfillment of God's redemptive plan. This chapter has explored the biblical foundations, theological implications, and practical applications of the promise of a new heaven and new earth, providing guidance and encouragement for living in light of this glorious future.

How the Hope of the Future Impacts Present Living

The Christian hope of a future where evil is eradicated, and God's kingdom is fully realized profoundly influences how believers live in the present. This hope, rooted in the promises of a new heaven and new earth, provides motivation, direction, and strength to navigate the challenges of this world. This chapter explores how the hope of the future impacts present living, offering biblical foundations, practical applications, and transformative insights for believers.

Biblical Foundations of Future Hope

The Promises of God

The Bible is filled with promises that assure believers of a hopeful future. These promises provide a solid foundation for living with hope and expectation.

- Jeremiah 29:11 (KJV): "For I know the thoughts that I think toward you, saith the LORD, thoughts of peace, and not of evil, to give you an expected end."

- John 14:2-3 (KJV): "In my Father's house are many mansions: if it were not so, I would have told you. I go to prepare a place for you. And if I go and prepare a place for you, I will come again, and receive you unto myself; that where I am, there ye may be also."

The Assurance of Resurrection

The resurrection of Jesus Christ is the cornerstone of Christian hope. It assures believers of their own resurrection and eternal life, impacting how they live each day.

- 1 Corinthians 15:20-22 (KJV): "But now is Christ risen from the dead, and become the firstfruits of them that slept. For since by man came death, by man came also the resurrection of the dead. For as in Adam all die, even so in Christ shall all be made alive."

The Vision of the New Creation

The vision of a new heaven and new earth where righteousness dwells inspires believers to pursue holiness and live in accordance with God's will.

- 2 Peter 3:13 (KJV): "Nevertheless we, according to his promise, look for new heavens and a new earth, wherein dwelleth righteousness."

Practical Ways the Future Hope Impacts Present Living

Living with Purpose and Direction

The hope of the future provides believers with a clear sense of purpose and direction, guiding their decisions and actions.

- Philippians 3:13-14 (KJV): "Brethren, I count not myself to have apprehended: but this one thing I do, forgetting those things which are behind, and reaching forth unto those things which are before, I press toward the mark for the prize of the high calling of God in Christ Jesus."

Pursuing Holiness and Righteousness

Knowing that the future holds a place where righteousness prevails motivates believers to live holy and righteous lives now.

- 1 John 3:2-3 (KJV): "Beloved, now are we the sons of God, and it doth not yet appear what we shall be: but we know that, when he shall appear, we shall be like him; for we shall see him as he is. And every man that hath this hope in him purifieth himself, even as he is pure."

Engaging in Acts of Love and Service

The anticipation of God's kingdom inspires believers to engage in acts of love, service, and justice, reflecting the values of the future kingdom in the present.

- Galatians 6:9-10 (KJV): "And let us not be weary in well doing: for in due season we shall reap, if we faint not. As we have therefore opportunity, let us do good unto all men, especially unto them who are of the household of faith."

Enduring Suffering with Hope

The hope of the future gives believers strength to endure suffering and trials, knowing that their present struggles are temporary and will be overshadowed by future glory.

- Romans 8:18 (KJV): "For I reckon that the sufferings of this present time are not worthy to be compared with the glory which shall be revealed in us."

Sharing the Gospel

The assurance of future hope compels believers to share the gospel with others, inviting them to partake in the promises of God's kingdom.

- Matthew 28:19-20 (KJV): "Go ye therefore, and teach all nations, baptizing them in the name of the Father, and of the Son, and of the Holy Ghost: Teaching them to observe all things whatsoever I have commanded you: and, lo, I am with you alway, even unto the end of the world. Amen."

The Transformative Power of Hope

Renewing the Mind

Hope in the future transforms how believers think, providing a renewed perspective that aligns with God's promises and purposes.

- Romans 12:2 (KJV): "And be not conformed to this world: but be ye transformed by the renewing of your mind, that ye may prove what is that good, and acceptable, and perfect, will of God."

Strengthening Faith

Hope strengthens faith, enabling believers to trust in God's faithfulness and provision even when circumstances are challenging.

- Hebrews 11:1 (KJV): "Now faith is the substance of things hoped for, the evidence of things not seen."

Cultivating Joy and Peace

The future hope cultivates joy and peace in believers' hearts, providing a foundation of stability and confidence amid life's uncertainties.

- Romans 15:13 (KJV): "Now the God of hope fill you with all joy and peace in believing, that ye may abound in hope, through the power of the Holy Ghost."

Biblical Examples of Future Hope Impacting Present Living

Abraham's Faith

Abraham lived by faith, trusting in God's promises of a future inheritance. His hope in God's faithfulness shaped his actions and decisions.

- Hebrews 11:8-10 (KJV): "By faith Abraham, when he was called to go out into a place which he should after receive for an inheritance, obeyed; and he went out, not knowing whither he went. By faith he sojourned in the land of promise, as in a strange country, dwelling in tabernacles with Isaac and Jacob, the heirs with him of the same promise: For he looked for a city which hath foundations, whose builder and maker is God."

Paul's Mission

The Apostle Paul's ministry was driven by his hope in the resurrection and the return of Christ. This future hope empowered him to endure suffering and remain committed to his mission.

- 2 Corinthians 4:16-18 (KJV): "For which cause we faint not; but though our outward man perish, yet the inward man is renewed day by day. For our light affliction, which is but for a moment, worketh for us a far more exceeding and eternal weight of glory; While we look not at the things which are seen, but at the things which are not seen: for the things which are seen are temporal; but the things which are not seen are eternal."

The Early Church

The early Christians lived with an expectation of Christ's return, which influenced their communal life, generosity, and perseverance in faith.

- Acts 2:44-47 (KJV): "And all that believed were together, and had all things common; And sold their possessions and goods, and parted them to all men, as every man had need. And they, continuing daily with one accord in the temple, and breaking bread from house to house, did eat their meat with gladness and singleness of heart, Praising God, and having favour with all the people. And the Lord added to the church daily such as should be saved."

Practical Reflections on Living with Future Hope

ultivating a Hopeful Mindset

Believers are encouraged to cultivate a hopeful mindset by regularly reflecting on God's promises and keeping an eternal perspective.

- Colossians 3:1-2 (KJV): "If ye then be risen with Christ, seek those things which are above, where Christ sitteth on the right hand of God. Set your affection on things above, not on things on the earth."

Engaging in Spiritual Disciplines

Practicing spiritual disciplines such as prayer, Bible study, and worship strengthens hope and aligns believers' hearts with God's future plans.

- 1 Thessalonians 5:16-18 (KJV): "Rejoice evermore. Pray without ceasing. In every thing give thanks: for this is the will of God in Christ Jesus concerning you."

Building a Supportive Community

Being part of a faith community provides encouragement and accountability, helping believers to live in light of future hope.

- Hebrews 10:24-25 (KJV): "And let us consider one another to provoke unto love and to good works: Not forsaking the assembling of ourselves together, as the manner of some is; but exhorting one another: and so much the more, as ye see the day approaching."

Serving Others

Hope in the future motivates believers to serve others, reflecting God's love and advancing His kingdom on earth.

- Galatians 5:13 (KJV): "For, brethren, ye have been called unto liberty; only use not liberty for an occasion to the flesh, but by love serve one another."

Expository Study with Strong's Concordance

Hope ("ἐλπίς" elpis)

The Greek word "ἐλπίς" (elpis), Strong's G1680, means hope or expectation. It signifies a confident expectation of future blessings based on God's promises.

- Romans 8:24-25 (KJV): "For we are saved by hope: but hope that is seen is not hope: for what a man seeth, why doth he yet hope for? But if we hope for that we see not, then do we with patience wait for it."

Future ("μέλλω" mellō)

The Greek word "μέλλω" (mellō), Strong's G3195, means to be about to, intend, or to come. It often refers to future events or actions that are certain to occur.

- Hebrews 10:37 (KJV): "For yet a little while, and he that shall come will come, and will not tarry."

Comprehensive Commentary

The Impact of Future Hope on Present Living

The hope of a future where God's kingdom is fully realized profoundly influences present living. It provides a foundation for purpose, perseverance, and proactive engagement in God's work. This hope encourages believers to live with an eternal perspective, pursue holiness, serve others, and endure suffering with faith.

Living Out Future Hope in Daily Life

Believers are called to live out their future hope through intentional actions and attitudes that reflect God's kingdom values. This involves cultivating a hopeful mindset, engaging in spiritual disciplines, building supportive communities, and serving others.

The Transformative Power of Hope

The transformative power of hope enables believers to navigate the complexities of life with resilience and joy. It shapes their worldview, strengthens their faith, and motivates them to make a positive impact in the world.

The hope of the future profoundly impacts present living for believers. By understanding and embracing this hope, believers can live with purpose, pursue holiness, engage in acts of love and service, endure suffering with faith, and share the gospel. This chapter has explored the biblical foundations, practical applications, and transformative power of future hope, offering guidance and encouragement for living in light of God's promises.

CHAPTER 12

SUMMARY OF GOD'S GOODNESS AND THE PRESENCE OF EVIL

Summarizing the Relationship Between God's Goodness and the Presence of Evil

The coexistence of God's goodness and the presence of evil is one of the most profound and challenging questions in Christian theology. Throughout this book, we have explored various aspects of this relationship, examining biblical foundations, theological insights, and practical implications. In this concluding chapter, we will summarize the key points discussed, providing a cohesive understanding of how God's goodness and the presence of evil intersect in the Christian worldview.

The Nature of God's Goodness

God's Intrinsic Goodness

God's nature is inherently good, as evidenced by His creation, His actions, and His attributes. His goodness is perfect, unchanging, and forms the foundation of His relationship with humanity.

- Psalm 34:8 (KJV): "O taste and see that the LORD is good: blessed is the man that trusteth in him."

- James 1:17 (KJV): "Every good gift and every perfect gift is from above, and cometh down from the Father of lights, with whom is no variableness, neither shadow of turning."

God's Sovereignty and Holiness

God's goodness is closely linked to His sovereignty and holiness. As the sovereign Creator, He exercises control over all things, and His holiness sets Him apart from all evil and imperfection.

- Isaiah 6:3 (KJV): "And one cried unto another, and said, Holy, holy, holy, is the LORD of hosts: the whole earth is full of his glory."

- Romans 8:28 (KJV): "And we know that all things work together for good to them that love God, to them who are the called according to his purpose."

The Origin and Nature of Evil

The Fall and the Introduction of Evil

Evil entered the world through the disobedience of Adam and Eve. This original sin resulted in the fall of humanity, bringing sin, suffering, and death into creation.

- Genesis 3:6-7 (KJV): "And when the woman saw that the tree was good for food, and that it was pleasant to the eyes, and a tree to be desired to make one wise, she took of the fruit thereof, and did eat, and gave also unto her husband with her; and he did eat. And the eyes of them both were opened, and they knew that they were naked; and they sewed fig leaves together, and made themselves aprons."

The Consequences of Sin

The presence of evil is a consequence of sin, affecting both the natural world and human relationships. Sin distorts God's creation, leading to moral evil, natural disasters, and various forms of suffering.

- Romans 5:12 (KJV): "Wherefore, as by one man sin entered into the world, and death by sin; and so death passed upon all men, for that all have sinned."

The Role of Free Will

Human free will plays a crucial role in the existence of evil. God created humans with the ability to choose, and this freedom entails the possibility of choosing against God's will, resulting in evil actions.

- Deuteronomy 30:19 (KJV): "I call heaven and earth to record this day against you, that I have set before you life and death, blessing and cursing: therefore choose life, that both thou and thy seed may live."

God's Response to Evil

The Plan of Redemption

God's goodness is ultimately demonstrated in His plan of redemption through Jesus Christ. The cross is the central event where God confronts and defeats evil, offering salvation and restoration to humanity.

- John 3:16 (KJV): "For God so loved the world, that he gave his only begotten Son, that whosoever believeth in him should not perish, but have everlasting life."

The Work of the Holy Spirit

The Holy Spirit plays a vital role in empowering believers to resist evil and live righteous lives. The Spirit provides comfort, guidance, and strength in the face of suffering and moral challenges.

- John 14:26 (KJV): "But the Comforter, which is the Holy Ghost, whom the Father will send in my name, he shall teach you all things, and bring all things to your remembrance, whatsoever I have said unto you."

The Promise of Restoration

God promises a future restoration where evil will be eradicated, and creation will be renewed. The new heaven and new earth represent the fulfillment of God's redemptive plan, where His goodness is fully realized.

- Revelation 21:1-4 (KJV): "And I saw a new heaven and a new earth: for the first heaven and the first earth were passed away; and there was no more sea. And I John saw the holy city, new Jerusalem, coming down from God out of heaven, prepared as a bride adorned for her husband. And I heard a great voice out of heaven saying, Behold, the tabernacle of God is with men, and he will dwell with them, and they shall be his people, and God himself shall be with them, and be their God. And God shall wipe away all tears from their eyes; and there shall be no more death, neither sorrow, nor crying, neither shall there be any more pain: for the former things are passed away."

Practical Implications for Believers

Living with Hope and Purpose

The hope of a future free from evil provides believers with a sense of purpose and direction. This hope motivates them to live in a manner that reflects God's goodness and advances His kingdom on earth.

- 1 Thessalonians 4:16-18 (KJV): "For the Lord himself shall descend from heaven with a shout, with the voice of the archangel, and with the trump of God: and the dead in Christ shall rise first: Then we which are alive and remain shall be caught up together with them in the clouds, to meet the Lord in the air: and so shall we ever be with the Lord. Wherefore comfort one another with these words."

Pursuing Holiness and Righteousness

Believers are called to pursue holiness and righteousness, resisting the influence of evil and striving to live according to God's standards.

- 1 Peter 1:15-16 (KJV): "But as he which hath called you is holy, so be ye holy in all manner of conversation; Because it is written, Be ye holy; for I am holy."

Engaging in Acts of Compassion and Justice

Reflecting God's goodness involves engaging in acts of compassion and justice, addressing the needs of those who suffer and working to rectify injustices in society.

- Micah 6:8 (KJV): "He hath shewed thee, O man, what is good; and what doth the LORD require of thee, but to do justly, and to love mercy, and to walk humbly with thy God?"

Relying on God's Strength

In the face of evil and suffering, believers are encouraged to rely on God's strength, trusting in His faithfulness and provision.

- Philippians 4:13 (KJV): "I can do all things through Christ which strengtheneth me."

Theological Reflections on God's Goodness and Evil

The Mystery of Evil

While the presence of evil poses significant challenges to understanding, it remains a mystery within God's sovereign plan. Believers are called to trust in God's goodness even when faced with the complexities of evil.

- Romans 11:33 (KJV): "O the depth of the riches both of the wisdom and knowledge of God! how unsearchable are his judgments, and his ways past finding out!"

The Victory of Christ

The victory of Christ over sin and evil provides the ultimate assurance of God's goodness. Through His death and resurrection, Jesus has defeated the power of evil, offering hope and redemption to all who believe.

- Colossians 2:15 (KJV): "And having spoiled principalities and powers, he made a shew of them openly, triumphing over them in it."

The Role of Suffering

Suffering, while a result of evil, can serve as a means for spiritual growth and deeper reliance on God. Through suffering, believers often experience God's presence and grace in profound ways.

- 2 Corinthians 12:9 (KJV): "And he said unto me, My grace is sufficient for thee: for my strength is made perfect in weakness. Most gladly therefore will I rather glory in my infirmities, that the power of Christ may rest upon me."

The relationship between God's goodness and the presence of evil is complex and multifaceted. Throughout this book, we have explored various dimensions of this relationship, recognizing that while evil exists as a consequence of sin and human free will, God's goodness remains unassailable. God's redemptive plan through Jesus Christ, the empowering presence of the Holy Spirit, and the promise of a new heaven and new earth offer believers hope and assurance.

As believers navigate the challenges of a world marred by evil, they are called to live with purpose, pursue holiness, engage in acts of compassion and justice, and rely on God's strength. This understanding not only provides a framework for addressing the problem of evil but also empowers believers to reflect God's goodness in their lives and contribute to His redemptive work in the world.

Encouragement to Trust in God's Plan and Goodness

Trusting in God's plan and goodness can be challenging, especially when faced with the realities of evil and suffering. However, the Christian faith offers profound reasons to trust in God's sovereignty, wisdom, and benevolence. This chapter aims to encourage believers to place their trust in God's plan and goodness, providing biblical insights, theological reflections, and practical applications for daily living.

Biblical Basis for Trusting in God

God's Faithfulness

The Bible consistently highlights God's faithfulness to His promises and His people. Trusting in God's faithfulness provides a foundation for confidence in His plans.

- Lamentations 3:22-23 (KJV): "It is of the LORD'S mercies that we are not consumed, because his compassions fail not. They are new every morning: great is thy faithfulness."

God's Sovereignty

God's sovereignty assures believers that He is in control of all circumstances, working everything according to His purpose.

- Isaiah 46:9-10 (KJV): "Remember the former things of old: for I am God, and there is none else; I am God, and there is none like me, Declaring the end from the beginning, and from ancient times the things that are not yet done, saying, My counsel shall stand, and I will do all my pleasure."

God's Wisdom

God's wisdom is perfect and beyond human understanding. Trusting in His wisdom means acknowledging that His ways and thoughts are higher than ours.

- Romans 11:33 (KJV): "O the depth of the riches both of the wisdom and knowledge of God! how unsearchable are his judgments, and his ways past finding out!"

God's Love

God's love is the ultimate assurance of His goodness. His sacrificial love demonstrated through Jesus Christ provides the clearest evidence of His benevolent character.

- John 3:16 (KJV): "For God so loved the world, that he gave his only begotten Son, that whosoever believeth in him should not perish, but have everlasting life."

Theological Reflections on Trusting in God

The Mystery of God's Plan

While we may not always understand God's plan, we are called to trust in His wisdom and goodness. The mystery of God's plan invites us to humble faith and reliance on Him.

- Proverbs 3:5-6 (KJV): "Trust in the LORD with all thine heart; and lean not unto thine own understanding. In all thy ways acknowledge him, and he shall direct thy paths."

The Purpose of Suffering

Suffering, though difficult, can serve a greater purpose in God's plan. It can lead to spiritual growth, deepen our reliance on God, and enable us to comfort others.

- 2 Corinthians 1:3-4 (KJV): "Blessed be God, even the Father of our Lord Jesus Christ, the Father of mercies, and the God of all comfort; Who comforteth us in all our tribulation, that we may be able to comfort them which are in any trouble, by the comfort wherewith we ourselves are comforted of God."

The Assurance of God's Promises

God's promises provide assurance and hope, enabling believers to trust in His plan even in uncertain times. His promises are guaranteed by His unchanging nature.

- 2 Peter 1:4 (KJV): "Whereby are given unto us exceeding great and precious promises: that by these ye might be partakers of the divine nature, having escaped the corruption that is in the world through lust."

The Hope of Eternal Life

The hope of eternal life with God gives believers the perspective needed to trust in His plan. This hope transcends present difficulties and points to a glorious future.

- Titus 1:2 (KJV): "In hope of eternal life, which God, that cannot lie, promised before the world began."

Practical Applications for Trusting in God's Plan

Prayer and Communion with God

Regular prayer and communion with God strengthen trust in His plan. Through prayer, believers can express their concerns, seek guidance, and find peace.

- Philippians 4:6-7 (KJV): "Be careful for nothing; but in every thing by prayer and supplication with thanksgiving let your requests be made known unto God. And the peace of God, which passeth all understanding, shall keep your hearts and minds through Christ Jesus."

Meditating on Scripture

Meditating on God's Word reinforces trust in His promises and character. Scripture provides the truth needed to counter doubts and fears.

- Psalm 119:105 (KJV): "Thy word is a lamp unto my feet, and a light unto my path."

Fellowship with Believers

Fellowship with other believers offers encouragement and support. Sharing experiences and testimonies of God's faithfulness can strengthen trust in His plan.

- Hebrews 10:24-25 (KJV): "And let us consider one another to provoke unto love and to good works: Not forsaking the assembling of ourselves together, as the manner of some is; but exhorting one another: and so much the more, as ye see the day approaching."

Obedience and Faithfulness

Living in obedience to God's commands and remaining faithful in all circumstances demonstrate trust in His plan. Obedience reflects a heart that trusts God's wisdom and direction.

- 1 Samuel 15:22 (KJV): "And Samuel said, Hath the LORD as great delight in burnt offerings and sacrifices, as in obeying the voice of the LORD? Behold, to obey is better than sacrifice, and to hearken than the fat of rams."

Gratitude and Praise

Practicing gratitude and praise shifts focus from problems to God's goodness. A thankful heart recognizes God's blessings and reinforces trust in His care.

- 1 Thessalonians 5:18 (KJV): "In every thing give thanks: for this is the will of God in Christ Jesus concerning you."

Biblical Examples of Trusting in God's Plan

Abraham

Abraham's trust in God's plan led him to leave his homeland and journey to an unknown land. His faith was rewarded as God fulfilled His promises to make Abraham the father of many nations.

- Genesis 12:1-4 (KJV): "Now the LORD had said unto Abram, Get thee out of thy country, and from thy kindred, and from thy father's house, unto a land that I will shew thee: And I will make of thee a great nation, and I will bless thee, and make thy name great; and thou shalt be a blessing: And I will bless them that bless thee, and curse him that curseth thee: and in thee shall all families of the earth be blessed. So Abram departed, as the LORD had spoken unto him; and Lot went with him: and Abram was seventy and five years old when he departed out of Haran."

Joseph

Joseph's life exemplifies trusting in God's plan amid adversity. Despite being sold into slavery and unjustly imprisoned, Joseph remained faithful, and God ultimately elevated him to a position of great influence.

- Genesis 50:20 (KJV): "But as for you, ye thought evil against me; but God meant it unto good, to bring to pass, as it is this day, to save much people alive."

Job

Job's unwavering trust in God, despite immense suffering, highlights the importance of faithfulness. His story demonstrates that God's plans and purposes transcend human understanding.

- Job 13:15 (KJV): "Though he slay me, yet will I trust in him: but I will maintain mine own ways before him."

Mary

Mary, the mother of Jesus, displayed profound trust in God's plan when she accepted the angel Gabriel's message. Her faith and submission to God's will had a pivotal role in the salvation narrative.

- Luke 1:38 (KJV): "And Mary said, Behold the handmaid of the Lord; be it unto me according to thy word. And the angel departed from her."

Paul

The Apostle Paul trusted in God's plan despite facing numerous hardships, including imprisonment, beatings, and shipwrecks. His letters often emphasize the joy and contentment found in trusting God.

- Philippians 4:11-13 (KJV): "Not that I speak in respect of want: for I have learned, in whatsoever state I am, therewith to be content. I know both how to be abased, and I know how to abound: every where and in all things I am instructed both to be full and to be hungry, both to abound and to suffer need. I can do all things through Christ which strengtheneth me."

Encouragement for Believers

Trusting God in Uncertainty

In times of uncertainty, believers are encouraged to trust in God's unwavering goodness and sovereignty. God's plans are perfect, and His timing is always right.

- Isaiah 55:8-9 (KJV): "For my thoughts are not your thoughts, neither are your ways my ways, saith the LORD. For as the heavens are higher than the earth, so are my ways higher than your ways, and my thoughts than your thoughts."

Finding Peace in God's Presence

God's presence offers peace and reassurance. Believers can find solace in knowing that God is with them through every trial and triumph.

- Psalm 46:10 (KJV): "Be still, and know that I am God: I will be exalted among the heathen, I will be exalted in the earth."

Living Out

Faith Daily

Living out faith daily involves practical steps of obedience, worship, and service. Trust in God's plan is demonstrated through actions that align with His will.

- James 2:17 (KJV): "Even so faith, if it hath not works, is dead, being alone."

Embracing God's Promises

Embracing God's promises provides hope and strength. His promises are sure, and His faithfulness guarantees their fulfillment.

- Hebrews 10:23 (KJV): "Let us hold fast the profession of our faith without wavering; (for he is faithful that promised;)"

Trusting in God's plan and goodness is a cornerstone of the Christian faith. Despite the presence of evil and suffering, believers are called to place their trust in God's sovereignty, wisdom, and love. This trust is nurtured through prayer, meditation on Scripture, fellowship with other believers, and practical acts of obedience and gratitude.

The examples of faithful individuals in the Bible, such as Abraham, Joseph, Job, Mary, and Paul, provide inspiration and encouragement. Their lives demonstrate that God's plans are perfect, and His goodness prevails even in the midst of challenges. By trusting in God's plan and goodness, believers can navigate life with confidence, hope, and a sense of purpose, knowing that God is working all things together for their good and His glory.

Final Reflections on Free Will, Human Choice, and Divine Sovereignty

The interplay between free will, human choice, and divine sovereignty is a profound and often complex aspect of Christian theology. Understanding how these elements coexist and influence each other provides deeper insights into God's nature, human responsibility, and the unfolding of God's plan in the world. This chapter offers final reflections on these themes, summarizing key points and exploring their theological and practical implications for believers.

Free Will and Human Choice

The Gift of Free Will

Free will is a fundamental aspect of human nature, given by God to allow individuals the capacity to choose. This gift reflects God's desire for a genuine relationship with His creation, based on love and voluntary obedience.

- Genesis 2:16-17 (KJV): "And the LORD God commanded the man, saying, Of every tree of the garden thou mayest freely eat: But of the tree of the knowledge of good and evil, thou shalt not eat of it: for in the day that thou eatest thereof thou shalt surely die."

The Responsibility of Choice

With the gift of free will comes the responsibility of choice. Human decisions have real consequences, influencing one's relationship with God, others, and the world.

- Deuteronomy 30:19 (KJV): "I call heaven and earth to record this day against you, that I have set before you life and death, blessing and cursing: therefore choose life, that both thou and thy seed may live."

The Impact of Sin

The fall of humanity introduced sin into the world, corrupting human nature and impacting the exercise of free will. Despite this, individuals retain the ability to choose, and through Christ, can overcome the power of sin.

- Romans 5:12 (KJV): "Wherefore, as by one man sin entered into the world, and death by sin; and so death passed upon all men, for that all have sinned."

Divine Sovereignty

God's Absolute Sovereignty

God's sovereignty means that He is in complete control over all creation. His plans and purposes are unthwartable, and His will ultimately prevails.

- Isaiah 46:9-10 (KJV): "Remember the former things of old: for I am God, and there is none else; I am God, and there is none like me, Declaring the end from the beginning, and from ancient times the things that are not yet done, saying, My counsel shall stand, and I will do all my pleasure."

Sovereignty and Human Freedom

Divine sovereignty and human free will coexist in a manner that allows God's purposes to be fulfilled while respecting human autonomy. God's foreknowledge and omnipotence encompass human choices without negating their freedom.

- Proverbs 16:9 (KJV): "A man's heart deviseth his way: but the LORD directeth his steps."

God's Redemptive Plan

God's sovereignty is most clearly seen in His redemptive plan through Jesus Christ. Despite human sin and rebellion, God's plan for salvation and restoration continues to unfold according to His sovereign will.

- Ephesians 1:11 (KJV): "In whom also we have obtained an inheritance, being predestinated according to the purpose of him who worketh all things after the counsel of his own will."

Theological Reflections on Free Will and Sovereignty

The Mystery of Coexistence

The relationship between free will and divine sovereignty is ultimately a mystery that transcends human understanding. Both truths are affirmed in Scripture, inviting believers to trust in God's wisdom and goodness.

- Romans 11:33-34 (KJV): "O the depth of the riches both of the wisdom and knowledge of God! how unsearchable are his judgments, and his ways past finding out! For who hath known the mind of the Lord? or who hath been his counsellor?"

God's Grace and Human Responsibility

Salvation is a gift of God's grace, yet it requires a human response of faith and repentance. This dynamic illustrates the interplay between divine initiative and human responsibility.

- Ephesians 2:8-9 (KJV): "For by grace are ye saved through faith; and that not of yourselves: it is the gift of God: Not of works, lest any man should boast."

Living in the Tension

Believers are called to live in the tension between trusting in God's sovereignty and actively making choices that honor Him. This balance involves seeking God's guidance, obeying His commands, and relying on His providence.

- Philippians 2:12-13 (KJV): "Wherefore, my beloved, as ye have always obeyed, not as in my presence only, but now much more in my absence, work out your own salvation with fear and trembling. For it is God which worketh in you both to will and to do of his good pleasure."

Practical Implications for Believers

Trusting God's Plan

Believers can trust that God's sovereign plan is good and perfect, even when circumstances are difficult or unclear. Trusting God's sovereignty brings peace and confidence.

- Jeremiah 29:11 (KJV): "For I know the thoughts that I think toward you, saith the LORD, thoughts of peace, and not of evil, to give you an expected end."

Making Wise Choices

Recognizing the significance of free will, believers are encouraged to make wise choices that align with God's will and reflect His character.

- James 1:5 (KJV): "If any of you lack wisdom, let him ask of God, that giveth to all men liberally, and upbraideth not; and it shall be given him."

Persevering in Faith

Understanding that God is sovereign helps believers persevere in faith, knowing that God is working all things for their good and His glory.

- Romans 8:28 (KJV): "And we know that all things work together for good to them that love God, to them who are the called according to his purpose."

Embracing God's Grace

Believers are called to embrace God's grace, acknowledging that their ability to choose and act is empowered by God's enabling grace.

- 2 Corinthians 12:9 (KJV): "And he said unto me, My grace is sufficient for thee: for my strength is made perfect in weakness. Most gladly therefore will I rather glory in my infirmities, that the power of Christ may rest upon me."

The relationship between free will, human choice, and divine sovereignty is a profound and enriching aspect of the Christian faith. It highlights the depth of God's wisdom, the dignity of human agency, and the assurance of God's ultimate control.

Believers are encouraged to trust in God's sovereign plan, make choices that reflect His goodness, and rely on His grace in all things. This trust and balance bring a sense of peace, purpose, and resilience, enabling believers to live faithfully amid the complexities of life.

This chapter has provided final reflections on free will, human choice, and divine sovereignty, summarizing their theological significance and practical implications for believers. By embracing these truths, believers can navigate their spiritual journey with confidence, knowing that God is sovereign and His plans are perfect.